For Grade

3

Student

Ready, Set, Show What You Know®

Activities to Build Skills for the Ohio Achievement Tests

Name ______________________________

Written By:
Andrea Karch Balas, Ph.D.
Judy Cafmeyer

Show What You Know® Publishing

Published By:
Show What You Know® Publishing
A Division of Englefield & Associates, Inc.
P.O. Box 341348
Columbus, OH 43234-1348
614-764-1211

www.showwhatyouknowpublishing.com

Printed in the United States of America
09 08 07 20 19 18 17 16 15 14 13 12 11 10 9 8 7 6 5 4 3 2

ISBN: 1-59230-062-6

About the Authors

Andrea Karch Balas, Ph.D., is an educator and a scientist who has taught both in the traditional classroom and in nonformal educational settings, from kindergarten to adult. Andrea has presented her research on the teaching and learning of science both nationally and internationally. She shares her expertise in this field with Show What You Know® Publishing through the development of a Science Across the Curriculum format that is presently being used for workshops. Andrea received her doctorate in education from The Ohio State University and is currently the Science Coordinator in a private K–12 school. In addition to this book, Andrea is a co-author of the Ready, Set, Show What You Know® series for the Florida Comprehensive Assessment Tests (FCAT) for grades K–3 and the Ready, Set, Show What You Know® series for grades K–3 in Ohio.

Judy Cafmeyer has taught for 17 years in public and private schools from kindergarten to eighth grade. She is currently the supervisor for a Pre-K–8th grade instructional program. Judy also plans and presents teacher workshops related to Englefield and Associates, Inc., products. A graduate of The Ohio State University with a degree in elementary education, Judy has experienced education from various vantage points: as a teacher, as a representative on district curriculum committees, as a parent, as a volunteer, and as a school board officer. In addition to this book, Judy is a co-author of the Ready, Set, Show What You Know® series for the Florida Comprehensive Assessment Tests (FCAT) for grades K–3 and the Ready, Set, Show What You Know® series for grades K–3 in Ohio.

Acknowledgements

Show What You Know® Publishing acknowledges the following for their efforts in making this assessment preparation material available for Ohio students, parents, and teachers.

Cindi Englefield, President/Publisher
Eloise Boehm-Sasala, Vice President/Managing Editor
Mercedes Baltzell, Production Editor
Erin McDonald, Project Editor
Lainie Burke, Editor/Graphic Design
Jennifer Harney, Illustrator/Cover Designer

Content Reviewer:
Erica T. Klingerman

Table of Contents

Introduction

This workbook is designed to give you practice using skills that will help you prepare for the Ohio Achievement Tests.

It is very important that you read the directions carefully and do what the directions tell you to do. In this way, you will not only be preparing for the Ohio Achievement Tests, you will be reinforcing the good test-taking habits that your teachers taught you in previous grades.

There is a special certificate for you at the back of this book. When you have completed all of the pages in this workbook, write your name on the certificate and have your teacher or parent sign it too! This certificate congratulates you on your efforts and shows that you are becoming a proficient learner.

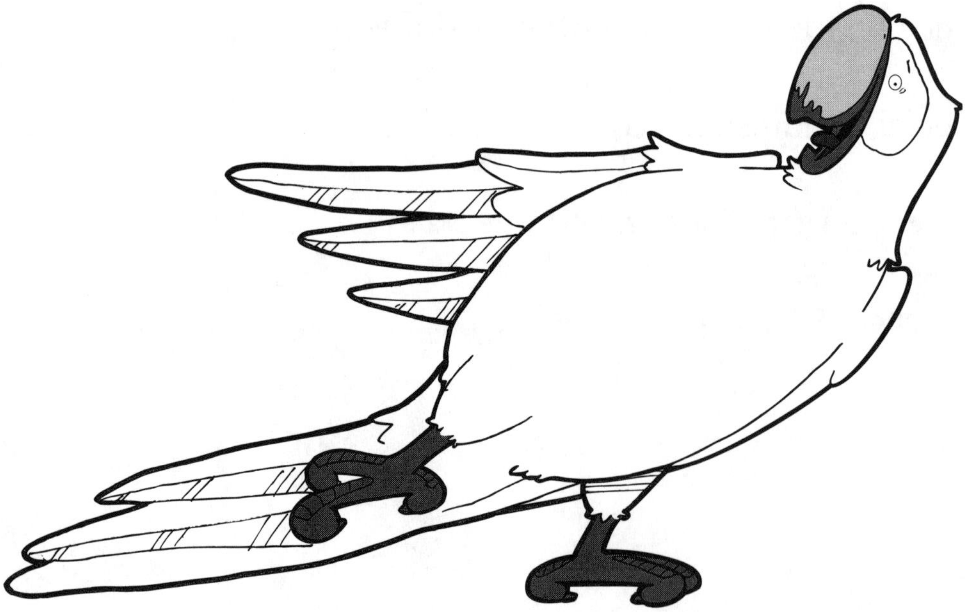

Writing

The Writing chapter of this workbook will help you continue building good writing habits. You will be practicing different skills that you are learning about in the writing process.

Good writing should always include:

- sentences that stay on topic.
- organized responses that have a beginning, a middle, and an end.
- a variety of words and sentences.
- the correct use of spelling, capitalization, and punctuation.
- handwriting that is legible (easily read by someone else).

Use this Writing Checklist to remind you to use good writing skills.

Writing Checklist

- [ ] I wrote about the topic.
- [ ] I wrote three or more complete sentences about the topic.
- [ ] I used a variety of words to make my writing interesting to read.
- [ ] I used simple, compound, and complex sentences in my writing.
- [ ] I checked my sentences for correct capitalization and punctuation.
- [ ] I used legible handwriting.

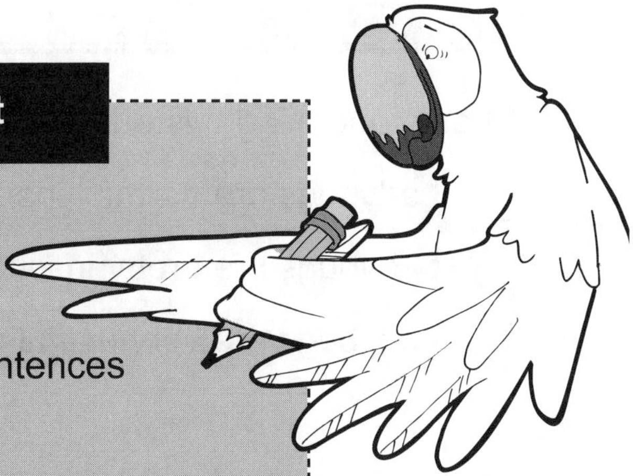

Directions: Read the passage about ladybugs below. Then, use a completely filled circle to answer the three questions about it.

Ladybugs 

Ladybugs are very useful insects. They help the environment by eating many insects that are harmful to plants. The ladybug finds plant lice and aphids to be tasty meals.

Some people believe ladybugs can even predict the weather. If you see a ladybug and repeat the question, "Ladybug, will Sunday be a nice day?" three times before it flies away, you will have fair weather for the weekend.

1. What is one thing this author wants you to know about ladybugs?
   - ◯ Ladybugs are harmful insects.
   - ◯ Ladybugs are pretty insects.
   - ◯ Ladybugs are very useful insects.

2. What is the author's purpose for writing about ladybugs?
   - ◯ to make you laugh at ladybugs
   - ◯ to tell you something about ladybugs
   - ◯ to make you like ladybugs

3. Which type of writing best describes this writing selection?
   - ◯ informational
   - ◯ persuasive
   - ◯ entertaining

Directions: On Monday, *The Belltowne News* ran the following article on the front page of the newspaper. On Thursday, two letters to the editor appeared in *The Belltowne News*. Read the article and the letters to the editor carefully. Then, answer the questions on the next two pages that relate to the information.

THE BELLTOWNE NEWS

vol. 282 Monday, July 9, 2003

New Police Station 4 Belltowne Park 0

The Belltowne City Council voted 4–0 to build a new police station. The site for the new building is located behind the old police station. The problem is that this land is also the Belltowne City Park. The baseball diamond and the picnic grounds will be cleared to make room for the new police station.

To the editor,

Belltowne's population has doubled in the last five years. This is the best city in the state! We need to have a bigger police station because we need more police officers to protect the community. We don't need the ball diamond at the city park. There are three ball diamonds at the high school for people to use.

Sincerely,
Mr. G. Brown

To the editor,

There is only one city park in Belltowne. My family and I enjoy picnics and ball games there during the summer. Destroying the park for a new police station is a terrible idea! I think you should find a different place to build your police station.

Sincerely,
Jake

Directions: Read Mr. Brown's letter to the editor and Jake's letter to the editor. Use the information from page 3 to help you answer the following questions. Use complete sentences for your responses.

1. Why did Mr. Brown write a letter to the editor of *The Belltowne News*?

____

____

____

2. What was Jake's purpose for writing a letter to the editor of *The Belltowne News*?

____

____

____

3. Who is the audience for these letters to the editor of *The Belltowne News*?

____

____

____

The **audience** refers to the person or group of people reading or hearing a piece of writing.

4. Which letter to the editor shows how you might feel about building a new police station on park land?

   ◯ Jake's ◯ Mr. Brown's ◯ neither

   Explain your answer choice using complete sentences with supporting details.

Directions: Mrs. Kerry's class was providing many ideas for writing paragraphs. Mrs. Kerry reminded the students that they should be very specific about their writing topics. She drew a flowchart on the board to illustrate how students can narrow their topics from broad to specific. A student suggested animals as a topic. Look at the flowchart to see how the teacher separated animals into two topics: wild animals and tame animals. The topic of wild animals was completed to give the students an example to follow.

Fill in the missing information about tame animals. Then, write a main idea for your topic in the space provided.

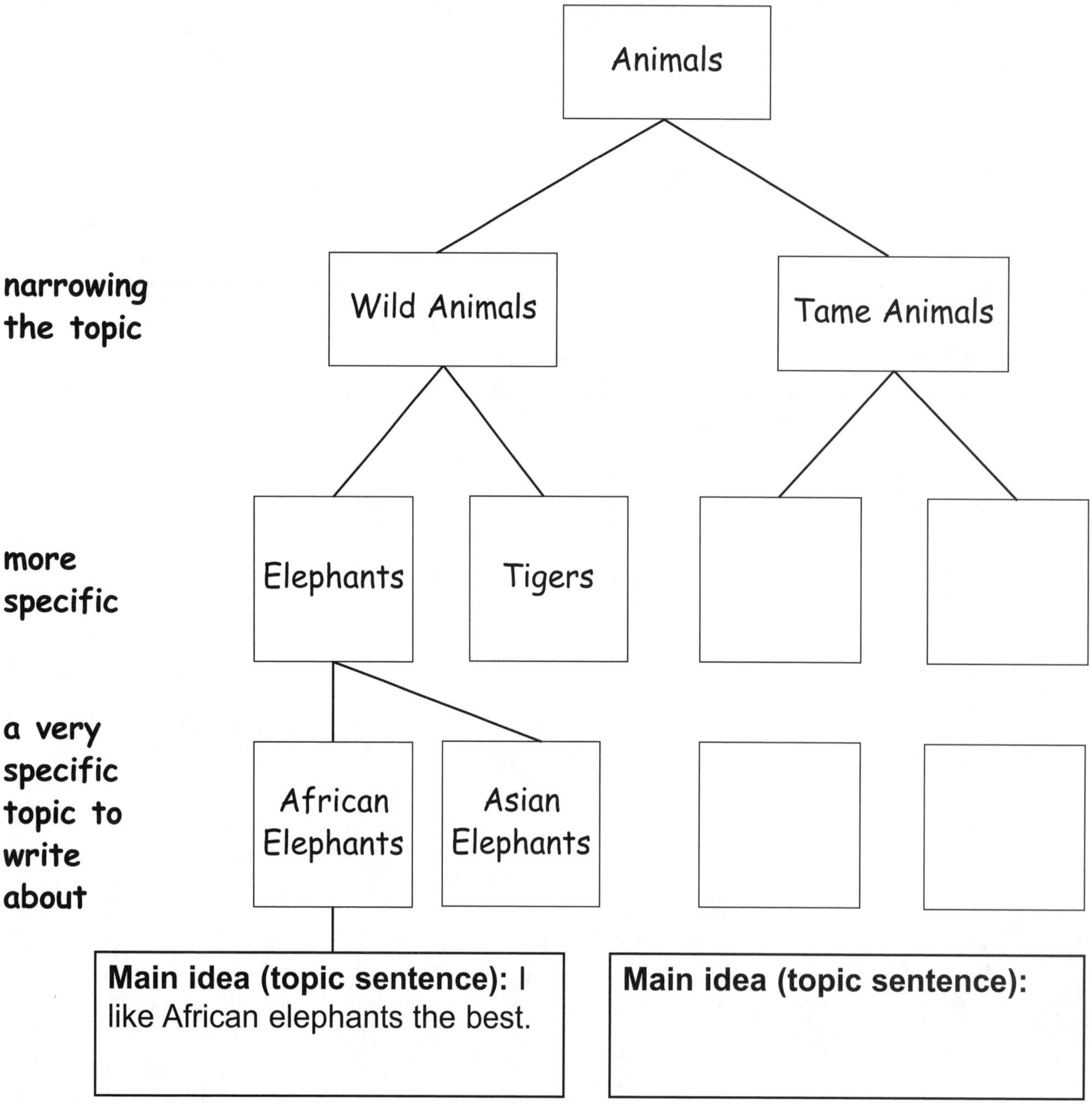

Directions: Use the topic from page 6 or another topic you would like to write about to complete the graphic organizer below.

Introduction—topic sentence

____

____

____

Body—give supporting details

____

____

____

Ending sentence—statement that brings the paragraph to a close

____

____

____

Directions: Will, Jordan, and Marla are writing paragraphs about their favorite birds—macaws. Will's paragraph tells about the macaw's appearance. Jordan's paragraph tells about macaws being good pets. Marla's paragraph tells about the way macaws act. Read each student's topic sentence (main idea). Then, use a completely filled circle to select the information that supports each topic.

Will's topic sentence (main idea):

Macaws are beautiful and colorful tropical birds.

A. ○ Macaws like baths.
○ Macaws are good pets.
○ Macaws come in many different colors.

B. ○ Macaws can learn to talk.
○ Smaller macaws are mostly green.
○ Macaws like to solve puzzles.

Marla's topic sentence (main idea):

Macaws are curious and intelligent birds.

C. ○ Smaller macaws are mostly green.
○ Macaws are beautiful birds.
○ Macaws can unlock their cages.

D. ○ Macaws are loyal and loving.
○ Macaws like interlocking toys.
○ Macaws need a lot of attention.

Jordan's topic sentence (main idea):

Macaws make good pets.

E. ○ Macaws can unlock their cages.
○ Smaller macaws are mostly green.
○ Macaws are loyal and loving.

F. ○ Macaws like baths.
○ Macaws like a lot of attention.
○ Macaws are curious.

Directions: Rewrite the two sentences you selected from the paragraphs written by Will, Jordan, and Marla on the previous page to form compound sentences. Be sure to use a connecting word when you combine the two sentences.

1. ____

____

____

____

2. ____

____

____

____

3. ____

____

____

____

____

Directions: Rewrite the thank-you note using correct capitalization and punctuation. Sign your name under the closing.

may 9 2004

dear aunt mary

thank you for taking me to the dayton museum of art last saturday i liked looking at the paintings

sincerely

Directions: Write a journal entry telling how third grade is different from second grade.

Directions: Use your best handwriting to rewrite the following paragraph. Be sure to correct the spelling of the underlined words.

Tamara <u>wuz</u> <u>filed</u> with excitement when she returned home <u>frum</u> her vacation. A <u>collectshun</u> of five new puppies was in the living room. To her amazement, she was told that she <u>kuld</u> keep <u>won</u> of the dogs as a new pet. She had to agree <u>two</u> some conditions. Tamara must handle the puppy carefully and feed it daily.

Directions: Write the correct spelling for the underlined words.

Tamara and to (1) frends (2) went on a picnic two (3) the park. Thay (4) put a stripped (5) blanket on the ground. Next, the three grils (6) unpackt (7) the basket. They ate there (8) lunchs (9) their (10). After lunch, they playd (11) on the swings.

1. ____________________
2. ____________________
3. ____________________
4. ____________________
5. ____________________
6. ____________________
7. ____________________
8. ____________________
9. ____________________
10. ____________________
11. ____________________

Directions: Rewrite the words in the left column using the *-ing* suffix. Remember the rules!

1. stop ____________________
2. charge ____________________
3. amuse ____________________
4. carry ____________________
5. map ____________________
6. mix ____________________

Directions: Rewrite the words in the left column using the *-ed* suffix. Remember the rules!

1. trap ____________________
2. serve ____________________
3. reward ____________________
4. pin ____________________
5. rip ____________________
6. learn ____________________

Directions: Use a completely filled circle to show the type of sentence and the punctuation mark needed to complete it.

Declarative	— statement
Exclamatory	— emotion
Imperative	— command
Interrogative	— question

	Declarative .	Exclamatory !	Imperative .	Interrogative ?
1. Please close the door	○	○	○	○
2. Are you finished reading the book	○	○	○	○
3. Hurray for Marty	○	○	○	○
4. The fox ran into the woods	○	○	○	○
5. Be very careful when you go in there	○	○	○	○
6. Who ate the last piece of cake	○	○	○	○
7. Dad will fix my bike on Saturday	○	○	○	○
8. Why are they laughing	○	○	○	○
9. When will the game begin	○	○	○	○
10. There are fifty stars on the flag	○	○	○	○
11. Take this note to the principal	○	○	○	○
12. The music concert was terrific	○	○	○	○
13. Our class won the writing contest	○	○	○	○
14. A clown performed at the circus	○	○	○	○
15. We are going to the museum on Tuesday	○	○	○	○

Directions: Rewrite each of the following sentences using the correct quotation marks, capitalization, apostrophes, and end punctuation marks.

1. ben lives on mulberry street in akron ohio

2. rosie asked are you going to michigan on october 4th

3. mr granger is the principal of suncrest elementary school

4. hurray ms browns class won a field trip to the cincinnati zoo

Directions: Read each sentence carefully. Use a completely filled circle to choose the correct pronoun that agrees with the noun or nouns in the sentence. The first one has been done for you.

1. Mary put ______ books on the desk.

   ○ his ● her ○ its

2. Jonah likes making dinner for ______ family.

   ○ his ○ her ○ their

3. Sheri and Alice worked on ______ projects.

   ○ her ○ their ○ its

4. Put the book back on ______ shelf.

   ○ her ○ their ○ its

5. The choir sang ______ songs.

   ○ its ○ her ○ his

6. I sent my aunt a card for ______ birthday.

   ○ his ○ her ○ its

7. The boys played in ______ own yard.

   ○ his ○ its ○ their

8. The students ate ______ lunches at 11:45 a.m.

   ○ his ○ her ○ their

Directions: The following six sentences are written in the present tense. Use the space provided to rewrite the sentences in the past and future tense. Write the sentences legibly in cursive and use spaces between the words.

1. Jess <u>feeds</u> the tropical fish every morning at 8 a.m.

   past tense: ______________________________

   ____

   ____

   future tense: ______________________________

   ____

   ____

2. Marshall <u>carries</u> the flag in the parade.

   past tense: ______________________________

   ____

   ____

   future tense: ______________________________

   ____

   ____

3. Latisha skips to her friend's house after school.

past tense: ______________________________

____

____

future tense: ______________________________

____

____

4. Daniel sweeps the garage on Saturday.

past tense: ______________________________

____

____

future tense: ______________________________

____

____

5. He <u>passes</u> the old, white house on his way to the park.

past tense: ______________________________

____

____

future tense: ______________________________

____

____

6. Theresa <u>writes</u> the letter to her grandmother.

past tense: ______________________________

____

____

future tense: ______________________________

____

____

Directions: Look at the following word phrases. Use a completely filled circle to select the correct personal pronoun to replace the underlined noun.

1. Henry's bicycle
   - ◯ his
   - ◯ her
   - ◯ its

2. Martha and Mary's lemonade stand
   - ◯ her
   - ◯ his
   - ◯ their

3. the table's leg
   - ◯ their
   - ◯ its
   - ◯ her

4. the neighbors' dog
   - ◯ her
   - ◯ his
   - ◯ their

5. my family's trip
   - ◯ her
   - ◯ our
   - ◯ his

6. Serena's tennis racket
   - ◯ her
   - ◯ his
   - ◯ their

7. the crowd's cheer
   - ◯ its
   - ◯ their
   - ◯ our

8. the book's raggedy cover
   - ◯ their
   - ◯ his
   - ◯ its

Directions: Marci read *Mr. Popper's Penguins* for a class report. It sparked her interest to learn more about penguins, for example, their habitats, different geographic locations, dietary needs, and life cycles.

Marci used a variety of sources to gather her research information: the public library, the local zoo, and the computer lab. Read each statement carefully, then decide where Marci found the information.

1. She searched for an Emperor penguin website during class.

   ○ public library ○ local zoo ○ computer lab

2. Marci reserved a *National Geographic* magazine that had an article about tropical penguins.

   ○ public library ○ local zoo ○ computer lab

3. Marci's science teacher loaned her a CD-ROM about penguin life cycles.

   ○ public library ○ local zoo ○ computer lab

4. While on a school field trip, Marci asked the guide how long it takes for penguin eggs to hatch.

   ○ public library ○ local zoo ○ computer lab

5. List three informational sources that Marci could use to find information about penguins:

   a. ______________________________

   b. ______________________________

   c. ______________________________

Directions: The students in Room 303 are studying family histories. The teacher took a class survey to find out which continents the students' ancestors came from. The results of the survey are shown on the table below. Refer to this table to fill in the chart that will list the number of students who have ancestors from different continents. Use numbers to complete the chart.

Class Ancestor Survey

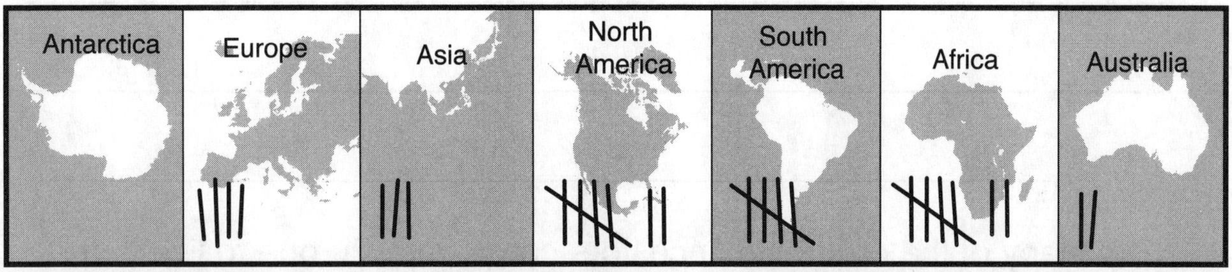

Continent	Number of Students
North America	______
Africa	______
South America	______
Europe	______
Asia	______
Australia	______
Antarctica	______

Directions: Refer to the chart on the previous page to answer the four questions about it. Write your answer in a complete sentence.

1. From which continents did most of the children's ancestors come to live in the United States?

____

____

____

2. How many of the children's ancestors came from Europe to live in the United States?

____

____

____

3. From which continent did the least number of the children's ancestors come to live in the United States?

____

____

____

4. Write another piece of information that the Class Ancestor survey tells you.

____

____

____

Directions: Refer to the article and the letters to the editor in *The Belltowne News* on page 3. Mr. Brown and Jake tried to persuade the readers by stating a personal opinion. Refer to the newspaper article and the letters to decide if each of the following sentences is a fact, Mr. Brown's opinion, or Jake's opinion. Use a completely filled circle to mark your answer choice.

	fact	Mr. Brown's opinion	Jake's opinion
1. Belltowne's population has doubled in the last five years.	○	○	○
2. We need to have a bigger police station because we need more police officers to protect the community.	○	○	○
3. There are three ball diamonds available for use at the high school.	○	○	○
4. There is only one city park in Belltowne.	○	○	○
5. Destroying the park for a new police station is a terrible idea!	○	○	○
6. I think you should find a different place to build the new police station.	○	○	○
7. This is the best city in the state!	○	○	○
8. The vote was 4–0.	○	○	○

Directions: Read the story below. Then, answer the questions about it. Use a completely filled circle to mark your answer choice.

Mrs. Hay's class is learning about family customs and traditions. Each student is preparing a short talk about a family custom or tradition. Martin is preparing the following talk for his class.

My Family's Special Dessert

I am going to tell you about my family's special dessert. It is a salad made with the favorite fruit of each member of my family. My dad likes plums. My mom likes strawberries best. My Uncle Frank and my older sister, Kim, like bananas. My favorite fruit is apples. Everyone in my family likes red grapes, so we add them to the dessert, too! When we have this at the end of our meal, there is never any left over.

1. Why is Martin preparing this talk for the class?
   - ○ to persuade the class to like this dessert
   - ○ to inform the class about his family's special dessert
   - ○ to tell about the history of desserts

2. What is Martin's favorite fruit?
   - ○ apples
   - ○ grapes
   - ○ plums

3. Which fruit do two people like best?
   - ○ green grapes
   - ○ bananas
   - ○ strawberries

4. Why are grapes added to the dessert?

   ◯ Grapes are red. ◯ Grapes taste good. ◯ Everyone likes grapes.

5. Martin wants to use a visual aid in his presentation. Which of the following would be the best choice?

   ◯ pictograph ◯ Venn diagram ◯ line graph

6. Explain your response to question 5.

Reading

The Reading chapter of this workbook provides activities to help you obtain information from different types of written resources:

- stories,
- poems,
- charts,
- tables, and
- graphs.

You are asked to read, refer, and respond to various fiction and nonfiction passages by filling in a circle for multiple-choice questions, writing a short answer (using a word phrase or one sentence), or writing an extended response (using several sentences and giving more supporting details to explain your answers).

Use this Reading Checklist to help you understand the reading passages and complete the workbook pages in this chapter.

Reading Checklist

- ☐ I read the directions on the page.
- ☐ I read the passages carefully.
- ☐ I circled words or phrases that I did not know.
- ☐ I reread the passage using context clues to help me understand the reading selection.
- ☐ I identifed different types of literature selections.
- ☐ I answered all the questions on the page.

Directions: Read the couplets below. Choose the rhyming word that completes each one. Use a completely filled circle to mark your answer choice.

1. In the third grade, the teacher taught
   About John Glenn, a famous Ohio ________.

   ◯ astronaut ◯ scientist ◯ engineer

2. The team is cheering the batter
   With loud, enthusiastic ________.

   ◯ cheers ◯ clapping ◯ chatter

3. Mary began to write
   About a dark and stormy ________.

   ◯ light ◯ night ◯ height

4. Katie and Kim looked in the sky
   To watch the big, fluffy clouds floating ________.

   ◯ over ◯ around ◯ by

5. Eating a healthy breakfast the day of a test
   Will help you to do your very ________.

   ◯ rest ◯ best ◯ pressed

6. Mrs. Jamison took her class
   To look for insects in the ________.

   ◯ grass ◯ trees
   ◯ bushes

A **couplet** is a two-line stanza in a poem.

Directions: Choose the correct letter to complete the word that solves each riddle. Use a completely filled circle to mark your answer choice.

1. You can fly me high in the sky on a windy day.

   ___ **ite**

   ○ k ○ b ○ m

2. My direction is the opposite of left.

   ___ **ight**

   ○ l ○ r ○ s

3. When I'm not on time.

   ___ **ate**

   ○ d ○ l ○ r

4. A homonym for me is right.

   ___ **ite**

   ○ l ○ t ○ wr

5. Put me on your foot. I have wheels.

   ___ **ate**

   ○ sk ○ sl ○ st

6. I am one of the five senses.

   ___ **ight**

   ○ t ○ h ○ s

Directions: Read the passage "A Symbol for Our Nation." Use context clues to write a short definition for each of the words listed below.

A Symbol for Our Nation

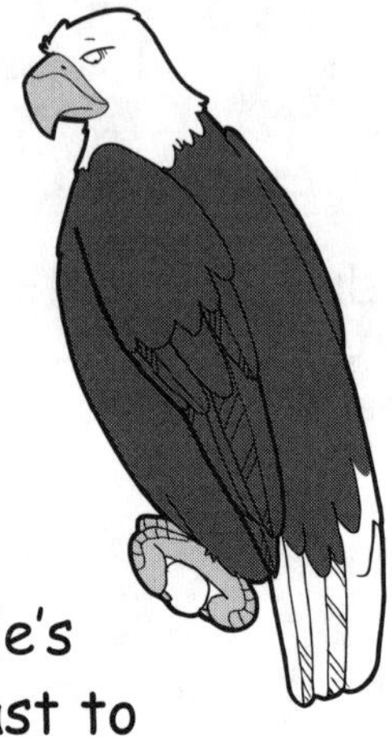

The bald eagle is a national symbol of the United States. This large bird of prey moves freely and has an outstanding appearance. It serves as a special model for our country.

The bald eagle is easy to recognize because it has unique physical characteristics. White feathers cover its head, neck, and tail. The eagle's dark brown body feathers give a striking contrast to its yellow eyes, beak, and feet.

1. national ______________________________

2. freely ______________________________

3. appearance ______________________________

4. physical characteristics ______________________________

5. contrast ______________________________

6. model ______________________________

Directions: Homophones are words that sound alike but have different meanings and spellings. Use a completely filled circle to select the homophone that fits the definition.

1.	used in cakes	○ flower	○ flour
2.	a vegetable	○ beat	○ beet
3.	a number	○ two	○ too
4.	an animal	○ hare	○ hair
5.	a facial feature	○ knows	○ nose
6.	the opposite of left	○ right	○ write
7.	an insect	○ bee	○ be
8.	fiction	○ tail	○ tale
9.	a highway	○ road	○ rode
10.	transportation	○ plane	○ plain

Directions: Use a completely filled circle to identify a synonym for the underlined word.

1. The boy put the box in the basement.

   ○ jar ○ crate ○ can

2. I tapped my foot to the beat of the music.

   ○ rhythm ○ sound ○ notes

3. My dad had to fix the wobbly porch steps.

   ○ concrete ○ wooden ○ unstable

4. She waved a bandana to start the race.

   ○ scarf ○ paper ○ sheet

5. Did you look at the book I gave you?

   ○ hear ○ glance ○ touch

6. Imagine you are on a spaceship going to Mars.

   ○ prove ○ pretend ○ provide

7. My mom's garden is lush with flowers.

   ○ filled ○ planted ○ picked

8. They laughed at the funny story.

   ○ chuckled ○ cried ○ choked

Directions: Read each sentence carefully. Then, use a completely filled circle to identify the antonym for each underlined word.

1. Jack turned <u>left</u> at the corner.

○ up ○ down ○ right

2. Her allowance was <u>increased</u> by fifty cents.

○ raised ○ decreased ○ under

3. Turn the lights <u>on</u>, please.

○ off ○ right ○ in

4. Was Jody <u>absent</u> yesterday?

○ early ○ late ○ present

5. The <u>girls</u> won the relay race.

○ team ○ boys ○ class

6. Maria ran <u>down</u> the hill.

○ up ○ under ○ around

7. When Tim arrived, the concert had just <u>begun</u>.

○ finished ○ started
○ opened

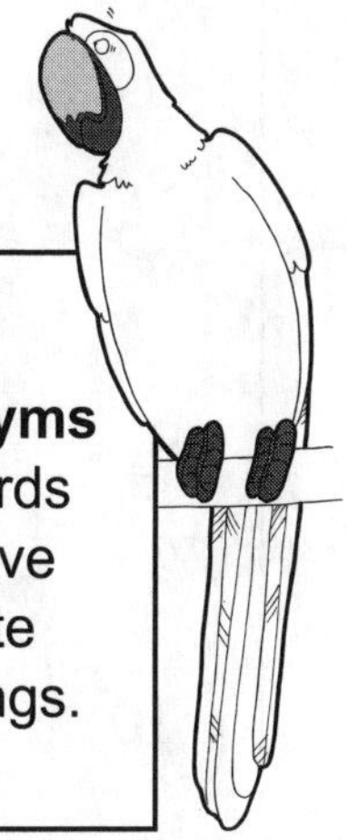

Antonyms are words that have opposite meanings.

8. He <u>forgot</u> to feed the fish before he went to school.

○ forgave ○ stopped
○ remembered

Directions: Match each word in the left column with a word in the right column to form a compound word. The first one has been done for you. Trace over the dashed line to practice matching the two words.

1. lady	fly
2. sun	drops
3. base	shine
4. butter	ball
5. rain	bug

Directions: Write the compound word for each picture.

6.  ______________________

7.  ______________________

8.  ______________________

9.  ______________________

10.  ______________________

Directions: Draw a line from the word phrase in the left column to its contraction partner in the right column.

1. I had	couldn't
2. it is	you're
3. could not	hasn't
4. would not	I'd
5. has not	it's
6. does not	I've
7. I have	haven't
8. you are	won't
9. have not	wouldn't
10. will not	doesn't

A **contraction** combines two words into one word. An apostrophe takes the place of the missing letters.

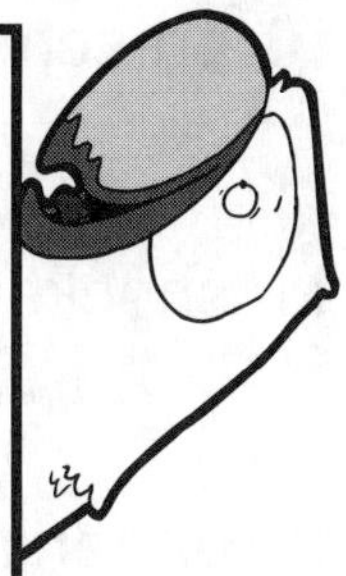

Directions: Look at the words in the left column. Each word has either a prefix (a syllable in front of the word) or a suffix (a syllable behind the word). Use a completely filled circle to show which one each word contains. Then write the root word for each. The first one has been done for you.

	prefix	suffix	root word
1. unhappy	●	○	happy
2. prettier	○	○	______
3. completely	○	○	______
4. thoughtful	○	○	______
5. reading	○	○	______
6. sleepiest	○	○	______
7. recycle	○	○	______
8. teacher	○	○	______
9. careless	○	○	______
10. preschool	○	○	______
11. checked	○	○	______
12. underline	○	○	______

Directions: Read each of the following sentences carefully. Find the root word for the underlined word. Use a completely filled circle to mark your answer choice.

1. The baseball game was very exciting.

   ○ excited ○ excite ○ excitement

2. The fastest runner finished the race first.

   ○ runs ○ running ○ run

3. The summer flowers smelled fresh.

   ○ smell ○ smelly ○ smells

4. Jamal's brownies were judged to be the tastiest in the bake sale.

   ○ tasty ○ tasted ○ taste

5. Carmen and Alyshia value their friendship.

   ○ friend ○ friends ○ friendly

6. Ben and his grandmother enjoy hiking on Saturday afternoons.

   ○ hikers ○ hikes ○ hike

7. The package arrived just in time for Sam's special day.

   ○ packed ○ packs ○ pack

8. The whole family came together for the celebration.

   ○ celebrate ○ celebrating ○ celebrates

Directions: Jack keeps a glossary of terms in his notebook as a reference. Here are some of the terms he uses often. Use Jack's glossary to find the term that is described in each of the following sentences. Write the term on the line given.

Glossary

compare - to show how two things are alike

contrast - to show how two things are different

fact - an actual happening or truth

graphic aid - any illustration, chart, map, table, diagram, etc., used to help interpret information about the text

inference - an important idea not directly stated in the text

opinion - a belief that might seem to be true but is not based on certainty

retell - restating the important events of a story, a poem, or an informational piece in your own words

summary - a statement that reflects the entire content of a text

1. Elise is rewriting the story in her own words. _______________
2. Manuel showed the difference between frogs and toads. _______________
3. Tabitha uses charts and graphs for her oral report. _______________
4. Sammy stated that Columbus is the capital of Ohio. _______________
5. Hannah told what the story was about in one sentence. _______________
6. Michael thought the movie was great. _______________

Directions: Mrs. Brown's class is learning to write sentences for specific purposes. The students are finding out that some writers use sentences to inform (tell something or state facts), to give directions (explain how to do something), or to entertain (appeal to the reader's personal interest).

Read each of the following sentences carefully. Is the purpose of the sentence to inform, to give directions, or to entertain? Use a completely filled circle to mark your answer choice.

1. Cynthia laughed when she read the comics.
   ○ inform ○ give directions ○ entertain

2. There are 12 girls in the class.
   ○ inform ○ give directions ○ entertain

3. Sue gave the class a recipe for making flatbread.
   ○ inform ○ give directions ○ entertain

4. Caterpillars turn into butterflies.
   ○ inform ○ give directions ○ entertain

Directions: Read the passages below about eagles and macaws. Select one of the birds and write a prediction about what you think might happen to that bird ten years from now. Fill in a circle to show which bird you are writing about.

○ The symbol of our nation, the bald eagle, was once in danger of becoming extinct. The efforts of many people have helped to protect the bald eagle from environmental dangers. The species is now thriving, and its numbers are increasing.

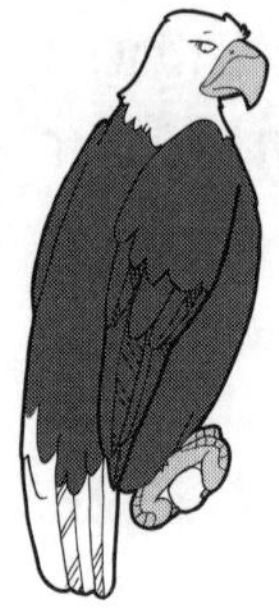

○ Macaws are an endangered species because their habitats are being threatened. Macaws like to nest high in dead trees. This helps to protect them from their predators. The trees that these birds use for nesting are being cut down every day.

____

____

____

____

____

____

____

Directions: Read the following information about ladybugs. The three reading passages show examples from Language Arts (poetry), Social Studies, and Science. Use the passages and what you know about these subjects to answer questions about them.

Language Arts

A Ladybug Poem by Treena

Ladybugs are very good to have around
When plants are growing in the ground.

Social Studies

The Ohio General Assembly voted the ladybug to be state insect in 1975.

Science

Ladybugs are actually beetles. The official name for a ladybug is Ladybird Beetle.

1. What do all of these reading passages have in common?

   ____

2. Which passage gives specific information about Ohio?

   ○ Language Arts ○ Social Studies ○ Science

3. Which passage is a rhyming verse?

   ○ Language Arts ○ Social Studies ○ Science

4. Which selection suggests that ladybugs are useful insects?

   ○ Language Arts ○ Social Studies ○ Science

5. Which selection tells about the official name for the ladybug?

   ○ Language Arts ○ Social Studies ○ Science

6. Which passage tells when the ladybug became the official state insect?

   ○ Language Arts ○ Social Studies ○ Science

Directions: Read the poem titled "Q. Marloe Beacher—Third-Grade Teacher" below. Then, answer the six questions about it on page 45.

Q. Marloe Beacher—Third-Grade Teacher
by Judy Cafmeyer

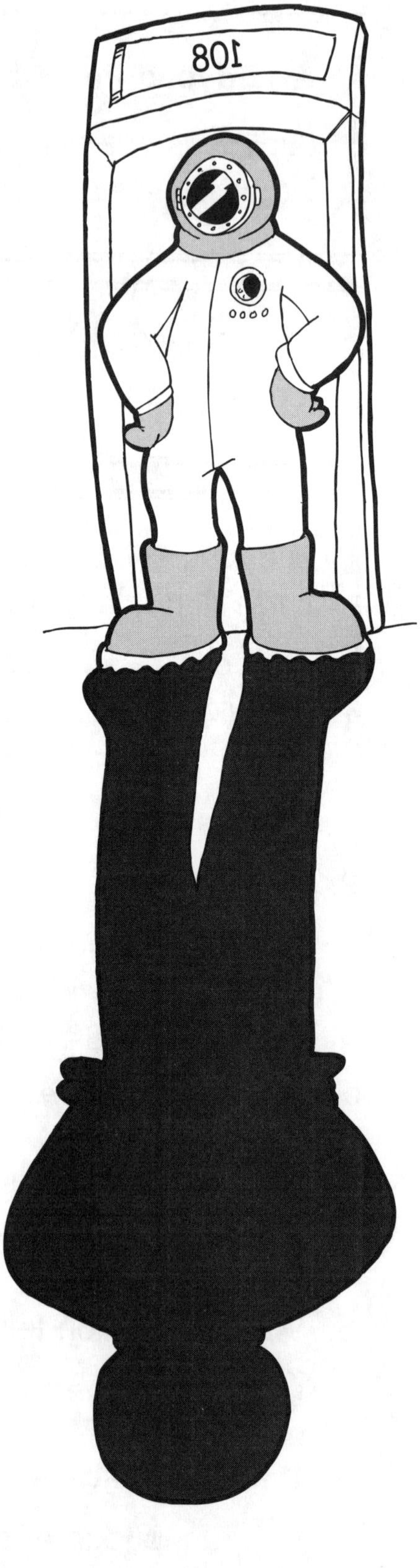

When the students arrived the first day in the fall,
They found a strange note attached to the wall.

No teacher to greet them, no one could be found.
The students were puzzled—just looking around.

But reading the note didn't help them much either.
"Are you ready for adventure? Are you a believer?"

Way too mysterious for the kids in Room 108,
This secretive note, and a teacher who's late?

It boggled their minds, causing major confusion,
Trying to come up with some logical conclusion.

An imposing shadow was cast on the floor,
As a curious figure appeared at the door.

On the head was a helmet, on the feet were some boots,
It was a strange-looking someone in an odd astronaut's suit.

Then came the announcement, "I am Q. Marloe Beacher,
Introducing myself as your new third-grade teacher."

Some students sat silent, some shocked and some dazed.
Still others were dumfounded, but all were amazed.

Then Q. Marloe Beacher said, "Hang on to your seats!
As we launch ourselves into some great learning feats."

Together we'll analyze, research, and explore
Interesting topics and subjects like never before.

From research and fractions to recycling a tree,
To learning about laws made in Ohio's General Assembly.

Now the launch pad is ready and all systems are "go"
For the exciting adventures we all want to know.

But, before we depart, let me remind you of one feature:
I am Q. Marloe Beacher, your new third-grade teacher!

Directions: Refer to the poem titled "Q. Marloe Beacher—Third-Grade Teacher" on page 44 to answer the following questions. Use a completely filled circle to show when each action happened—at the beginning, in the middle, or at the end of the poem—or to show that the action did not happen in the poem.

1. As a curious figure appeared at the door.

   ○ beginning ○ middle ○ end

2. Now the launch pad is ready and all systems are "go."

   ○ beginning ○ middle ○ end

3. They found a strange note attached to the wall.

   ○ beginning ○ middle ○ end

4. Some students sat silent, some shocked and some dazed.

   ○ beginning ○ middle ○ end

5. As I remove this helmet from the top of my head.

   ○ middle ○ end ○ did not happen

6. A shadow was cast on the floor.

   ○ beginning ○ middle ○ did not happen

Directions: Read the passage about ladybugs. Then follow the directions to complete the activity below.

Ladybugs can be very useful insects. They help the environment by eating many insects that are harmful to plants. The ladybug finds plant lice and aphids to be tasty meals.

The following sentence can be inferred from the paragraph:

Farmers and gardeners can benefit from ladybugs.

Underline the phrases or sentences in the paragraph above that support this inference, then rewrite the information in your own words on the lines below.

Directions: Below, you will find two major ideas and six supporting ideas. Three of the supporting ideas are related to major idea 1. Three of the supporting ideas are related to major idea 2.

Select one of the major ideas and write it in the "major idea" section on the next page. Then, circle the three supporting ideas that relate to the major idea you chose. Write these three supporting ideas in the appropriate sections on the next page.

Major Ideas

1. The macaw is a beautiful, colorful, tropical bird.

2. Macaws are curious and intelligent birds.

Supporting Ideas

A. A macaw can learn to eat with a spoon.

B. Interlocking toys can entertain macaws.

C. Macaws come in many different colors.

D. Larger macaws have feathers that are dark red, yellow, blue, and green.

E. Macaws can unlock their cages.

F. The smaller macaws are mostly green.

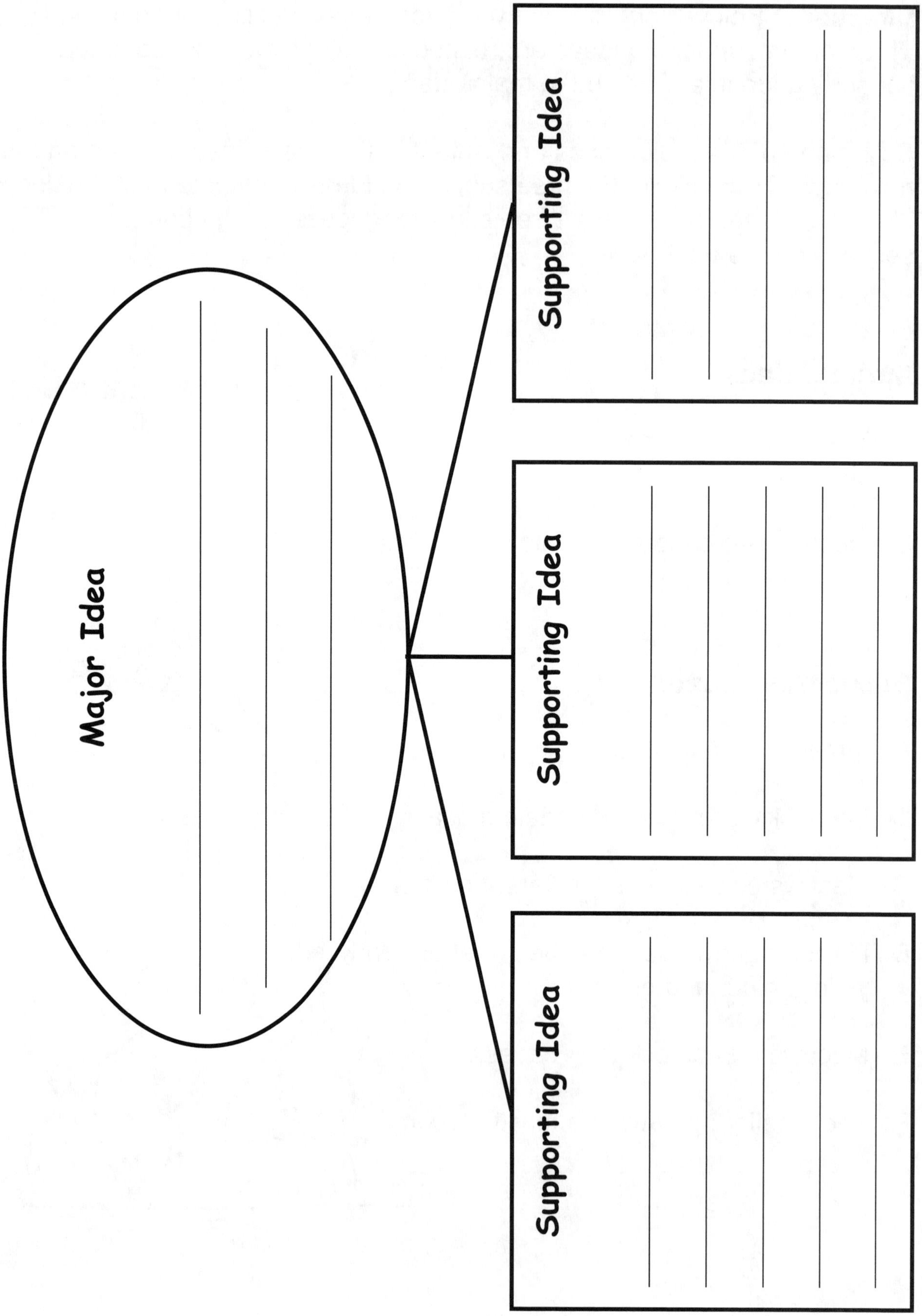
Major Idea
Supporting Idea
Supporting Idea
Supporting Idea

Directions: Read the story below. Then, answer the four questions about it. Use a completely filled circle to mark your answer choice.

Wanda is a new student at Sunshine Elementary School. The teacher, Mr. Smith, asked Wanda to write a story about herself for the class newsletter. He wanted Wanda to tell the students about herself.

Wanda's Story

My name is Wanda Tipton. I am eight years old. I lived in Florida before my family moved to Ohio. I have two older sisters, Claire and Beth, and a younger brother, Mickey. My dog's name is Buster. He is black and white. I like to swim and go hiking. I also like to read books about flowers and insects. My favorite color is blue.

1. Who asked Wanda to write the story?

   ○ Claire ○ Mr. Smith ○ Mickey

2. What is the main reason Wanda wrote this story?

   ○ to tell about Buster ○ to tell about Florida ○ to tell about herself

3. What do you know about Wanda?

   ○ She has 2 brothers and 1 sister. ○ She has 2 sisters and 1 brother. ○ She has 3 sisters.

4. Wanda wrote a story about herself. What kind of story is this?

   ○ autobiography ○ biography ○ science fiction

Directions: Use your own words to write definitions for the underlined words. Refer to the poem "Q. Marloe Beacher—Third Grade Teacher" on page 44 to help you understand the words in context.

1. a strange note <u>attached</u> to the wall

____

____

2. causing major <u>confusion</u>

____

____

3. a <u>curious</u> figure

____

____

4. Then came the <u>announcement</u>

____

____

5. to <u>analyze</u>, <u>research</u>, and <u>explore</u>

   analyze: ______________________________________

   research: _____________________________________

   explore: ______________________________________

Directions: Mr. Patrick asked each of his students to complete a book report. Michelle and Jared both read fictional animal stories. Here are their book reports. Use the reports to decide whose recommendation will help other students choose which book to read.

Michelle	Jared
TITLE: Fifty Fine Felines	**TITLE:** No Fleas, Please
AUTHOR: M. Calico	**AUTHOR:** Rough Ruff
MAIN CHARACTERS: Three cats named Sophie, Reggie, and Clarice	**MAIN CHARACTERS:** Two fleas named Bugsy and Rocco
SUMMARY: Fifty happy cats live like millionaires in a mansion outside New York City.	**SUMMARY:** The story tells the adventures of two fleas, Bugsy and Rocco, as they enjoy life on a St. Bernard named Bernice.
RECOMMENDATION: Thumbs up!	**RECOMMENDATION:** Thumbs up!

	Michelle	Jared	Both
1. Franco likes fiction stories about animals.	○	○	○
2. Rena enjoys reading books about cats.	○	○	○
3. Misti reads anything she can find about St. Bernards.	○	○	○
4. Meggie is curious about cats living in a mansion.	○	○	○

Directions: Read each sentence carefully. Select the best reason (enjoyment, literary experience, gain information, perform a task) to show why each child chose the independent reading materials.

1. Juan wanted to learn how to care for his goldfish.

   ○ enjoyment ○ literary experience ○ gain information

2. Marie can't wait to read the newest book by her favorite author.

   ○ literary experience ○ enjoyment ○ perform a task

3. This summer, Phillip plans to read a variety of literature—fiction, nonfiction, and poetry.

   ○ perform a task ○ literary experience ○ gain information

4. William wants to find out more about wing designs of airplanes.

   ○ enjoyment ○ perform a task ○ gain information

5. Jody found a recipe for oatmeal cookies.

   ○ perform a task ○ gain information ○ literary experience

Enjoyment – personal-choice reading materials

Literary experience – choosing different kinds of literature: novels, storybooks, poetry, etc.

Gain information – choose specific subjects for an information search

Perform a task – choose materials to complete an assigment or to learn a new skill

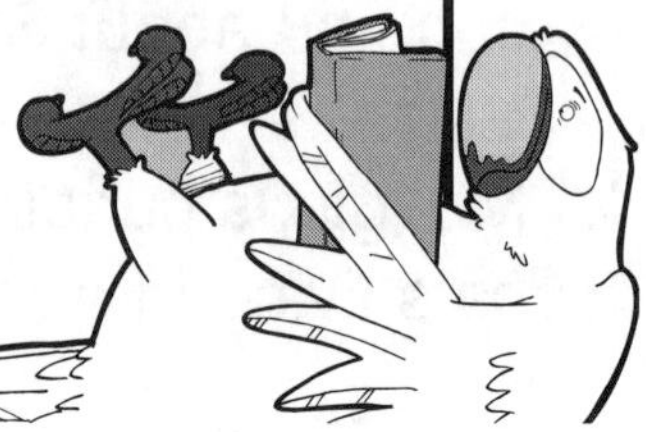

Directions: Use this Table of Contents to answer the questions below. Write a short-answer response on the lines provided.

Table of Contents

1. On which page can you find the Mathematics Checklist? page _______
2. Deana just finished page 27. What subject did the worksheet cover? __________
3. How many different subjects are covered in this workbook? __________
4. Matt has a Science worksheet to do. Which page begins the Science chapter? page _______
5. Vince completed all the worksheets in the book. Where is the Certificate of Completion? page _______

Directions: Read the story titled "Max, the Mischievous Macaw" below. Then, answer the six questions about it on page 55.

Max, the Mischievous Macaw
by Judy Cafmeyer

Billy knew the routine well. It happened almost every day. It was Billy's job to look for Max. Where would he find Max? What mischief had Max gotten into? Did Max destroy anything in the house? These were the questions Billy asked himself as he searched all the rooms looking for Max.

Macaws are well-known for enjoying puzzles, and perhaps Max saw picking the latch on his cage as a fun puzzle to solve. At first, it was easy to find Max because the macaw wasn't familiar with the new surroundings. The bird would stay near the cage, which stood in the corner of the dining room next to the kitchen. Billy usually found Max sitting on the kitchen counter with the remnants of a pretzel feast scattered around. Recently, however, Max had started exploring other areas of the house.

It was Max's curiosity that caused Billy's daily task to begin. He had to locate Max and hope the cleanup would be easy.

Directions: Read the story titled "Max, the Mischievious Macaw" on page 54 to answer the questions about it. Refer to the story to find the information you need. Write a complete sentence for your response.

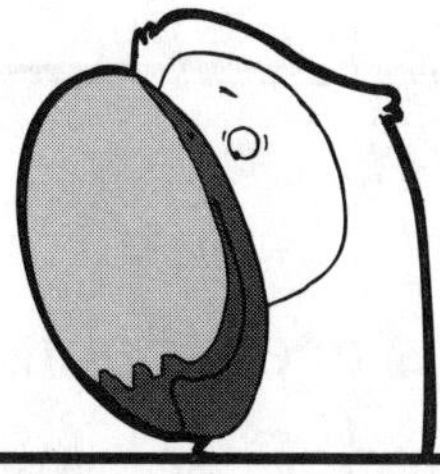

1. Who takes care of Max? ______________________________

____

2. What was found scattered around? ______________________________

____

3. Where is Max's cage? ______________________________

____

4. When did Max get into mischief? ______________________________

____

5. How did Max get out of his cage? ______________________________

____

6. Why do you think Billy cleaned up Max's mess every day? __________

____

____

Directions: Phillip wrote the following report about frogs for a science unit on pond life. Read Phillip's report carefully to answer the questions about it.

Frogs

Frogs are amphibians. They are animals that can live in water and on land. Frogs lay their eggs below the surface of the water. At first, the eggs look like tiny black specks. Then, these specks grow into tadpoles and finally into frogs. Adult frogs can live on land, but they must stay in wet places to keep their skin moist. The moist skin helps frogs absorb oxygen. Webbed feet help frogs move through water easily.

1. What is the main idea in this informational text?

   ○ Frogs begin as tadpoles. ○ Frogs are amphibians. ○ Frogs have webbed feet.

2. List three supporting details from the text.

   a. ______________________________

   b. ______________________________

   c. ______________________________

Directions: A class poll was taken to find which fiction books students liked. The results of the poll were put into a table for the class to analyze. Fill in a circle to indicate whether the information **can** or **cannot** be found using the Favorite Fiction table.

Favorite Fiction

Science Fiction	Adventure	Mystery	Fables, Tall Tales, & Legends	Series Novels	Animal Stories
𝍷𝍷𝍷	𝍸	𝍷𝍷𝍷𝍷	𝍷𝍷	𝍸 𝍷𝍷𝍷	𝍷𝍷𝍷

	can	**cannot**
1. The title of the class' favorite science fiction book.	○	○
2. The least favorite kind of fiction book.	○	○
3. The types of fiction books that interest boys.	○	○
4. Does this class enjoy reading animal books or adventure books more?	○	○
5. The total number of students that voted.	○	○
6. The class' favorite author of fiction stories.	○	○
7. Which types of books interest girls?	○	○
8. The teacher's favorite fiction book.	○	○
9. The fraction of the class that enjoys series novels and mysteries.	○	○
10. The ages of the students in the class.	○	○

Directions: Mandi found the following directions for making an ice cream sundae. The directions are not in the correct order. Help Mandi put the directions in the right sequence so she can make an ice cream sundae. Rewrite the correct order in the space provided.

Ice Cream Sundae

1. Coat ice cream with a syrup topping.
2. Enjoy your treat!
3. Put a cherry on the top.
4. Squirt whipped cream over topping.
5. Scoop ice cream into a bowl.

Ice Cream Sundae

1. ____________________
2. ____________________
3. ____________________
4. ____________________
5. ____________________

Directions: Read the story titled "Farmer Fo-Fum and the Beanstalk" below. Then, fill in the Venn diagram on page 61.

Farmer Fo-Fum and the Beanstalk
by Judy Cafmeyer

Once upon a time, there was a farmer named Jack who decided to plant some bean seeds. Over the years, Farmer Jack became very famous in Beantown for growing the tallest beanstalks in the county. In fact, for seven years in a row, Jack won the blue ribbon at the county fair for his tall beanstalks.

In the next town, there lived a farmer named Fe-Fi Fo-Fum who was tired of taking second place to Farmer Jack in the beanstalk contest. He decided once and for all that he was going to win the blue ribbon. He would not only grow the tallest beanstalk in the county, he would grow the tallest beanstalk in the world.

Farmer Fo-Fum went to his shed and started mixing different ingredients to feed his bean plant. Every day, he would add another strange blend to the plant. Soon, the plant was growing faster than he had ever dreamed it could. It grew taller than the tallest tree in the forest; then, it reached into the clouds and beyond.

One day, Farmer Fo-Fum went to check on his giant plant, feeling very sure that his plant would win first place at the county fair. It was certainly the tallest plant in the county, and it was possibly the tallest plant in the world! As Farmer Fo-Fum was admiring his prize plant, he noticed it looked somewhat like a ladder. He wondered if he could climb the beanstalk. He started up the step-like leaves of the beanstalk and climbed higher and higher until his shed looked like a speck of dirt on the ground.

When the judges arrived to award Farmer Fo-Fum the blue ribbon for growing the tallest beanstalk in the county (and possibly the world!), they couldn't find him, so they pinned the blue ribbon to the beanstalk.

"Where do you suppose he is?" asked one judge.

"I don't know," answered another judge. "He's probably climbing that giant beanstalk."

"Sure—that's a good one!" said the third judge. The three judges walked away, laughing.

Directions: Compare and contrast the traditional folktale "Jack and the Beanstalk" to the story "Farmer Fo-Fum and the Beanstalk" on pages 59–60. Use the Venn diagram to note similarities and differences between the stories.

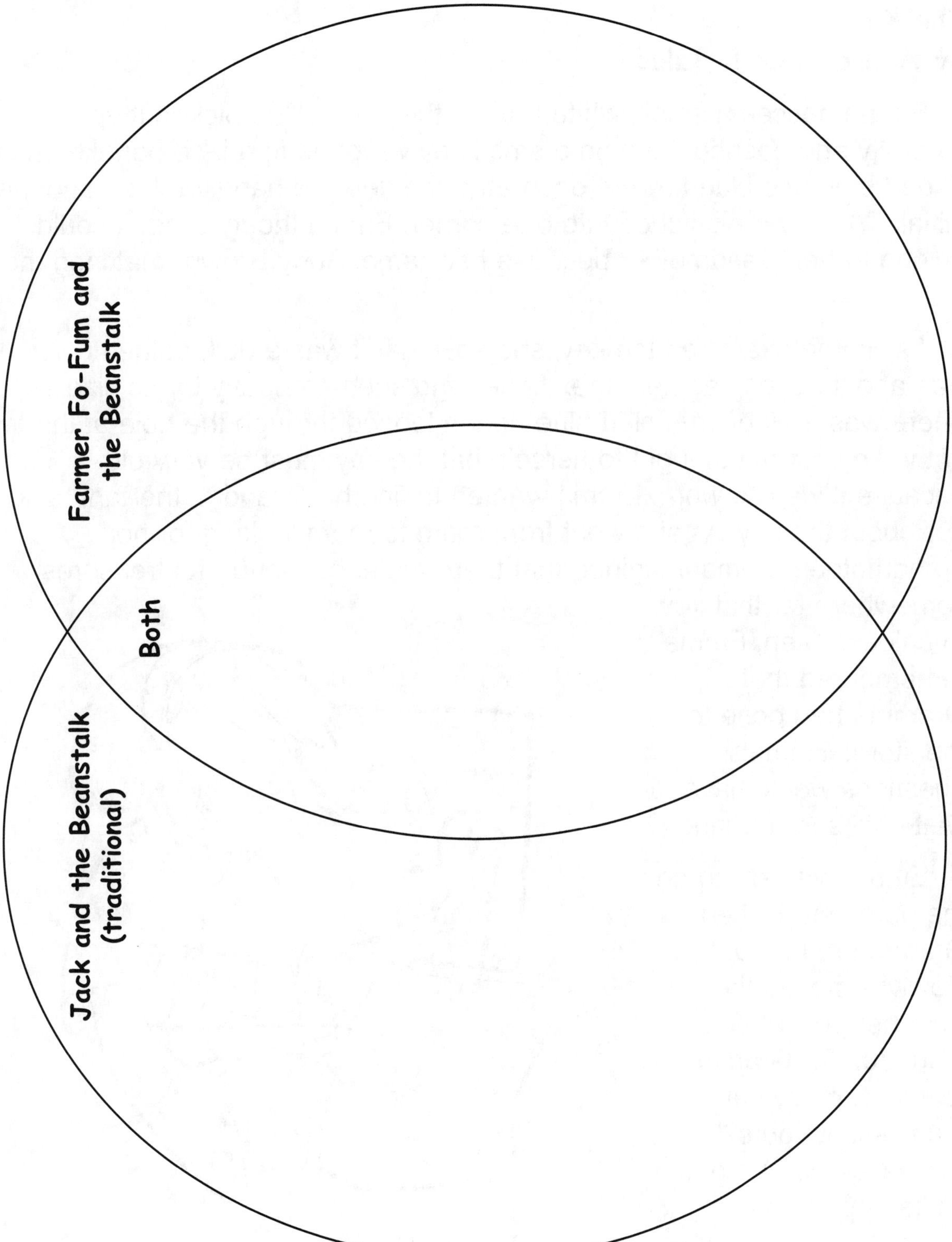

Directions: Read the story titled "The Key" below. Then, fill in the chart on page 63.

The Key
by Andrea Karch Balas

Emma noticed a small, white box on the stairs. She picked it up carefully and opened it to find a small key wrapped in a lace handkerchief. Faded pink and blue flowers decorated the delicate handkerchief, and the initials "A.B." were stitched into one corner. Emma thought that it could belong to her grandmother because her name, Abby Brown, matched the initials.

As Emma examined the key, she saw that it was a dull, golden color. It was about as long as her index finger and seemed heavy for its size. There was a bit of crumpled blue ribbon looped through the hole at the top of the key. Emma thought to herself that the key must be very old because it was so worn. Emma wanted to find her grandmother and ask her about the key. As she went from room to room looking for her grandmother, Emma imagined that there might be wonderful treasures somewhere for that key to unlock. Then, Emma remembered that Gramma had gone to the store. Emma's questions would have to wait until she returned.

Emma was sitting on the porch step when Gramma returned. She slowly removed the key from her pocket and held it up for Gramma to see. "Look what I found—is it yours?" Emma asked. A broad smile appeared on

Gramma's face as she inspected the key. "I thought I had lost this," Gramma said. "This key opens a very special box I have stored in the attic." Then, Gramma took Emma's hand and said, "Come with me. I have something to show you."

Emma and her grandmother walked through the house to the back stairs that led up to the attic. As they climbed the steep steps to the crowded storage place, Emma's mind raced with thoughts about that special box. She wondered what it would look like and, most importantly, what would be inside the box.

Directions: Provide three specific details about the key and the attic. For example, size, color, location, etc.

Key	Attic
1. ______________________	1. ______________________
______________________	______________________
2. ______________________	2. ______________________
______________________	______________________
3. ______________________	3. ______________________
______________________	______________________

Directions: Retell the plot sequence of the story titled "The Key" on pages 62–63. Use your own words to tell what happened first, next, and last. Write complete sentences for your responses.

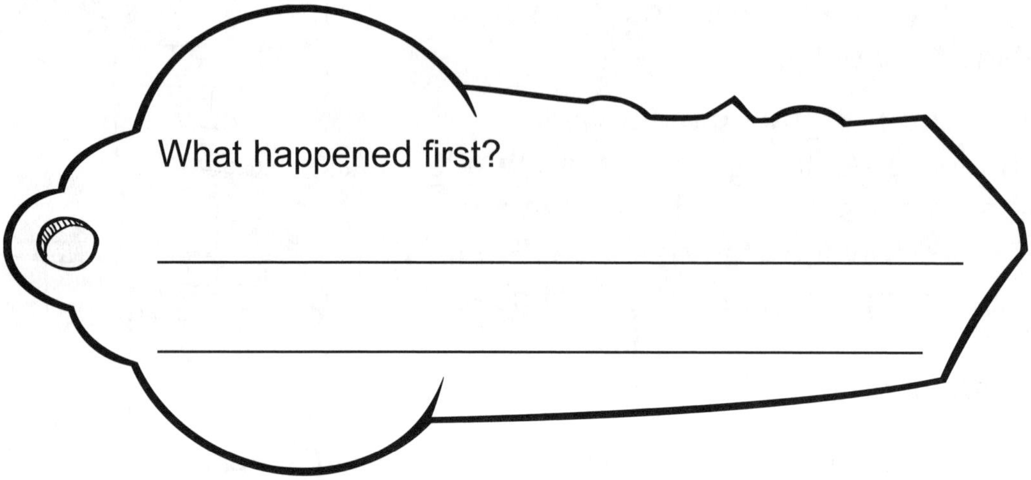

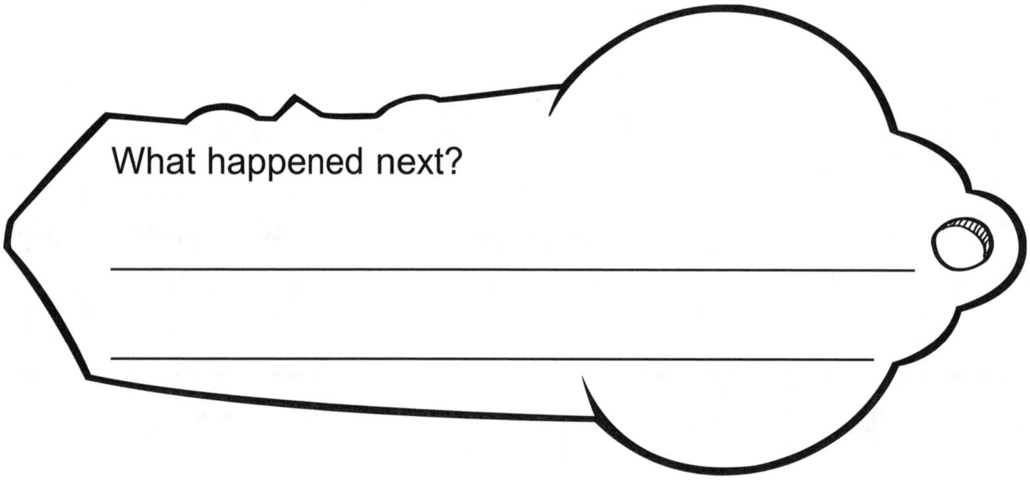

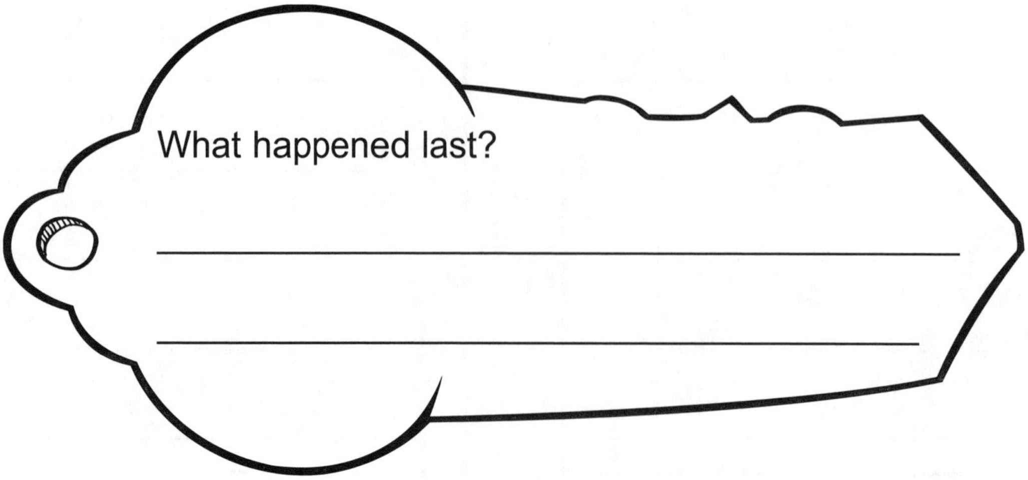

Directions: Refer to the story titled "Farmer Fo-Fum and the Beanstalk" on pages 59–60 to answer the following questions. After answering the question, explain why you answered the question the way you did.

1. What type of writing is this story?

   ◯ fiction ◯ nonfiction ◯ poetry

   Use complete sentences to explain your answer choice.

   ____

   ____

   ____

   ____

2. What is the main idea of the story?

   ◯ growing tall plants ◯ winning a blue ribbon

   Use complete sentences to explain your answer choice.

   ____

   ____

   ____

   ____

3. What is one thing that you learned from this story? Use complete sentences to explain your answer.

Directions: Read each sentence carefully. The sentences use words that appeal to the five senses: touch, taste, sight, hearing, and smell. Use a completely filled circle to select the correct sense in each sentence.

1. Mike enjoyed listening to the gentle patter of rain on the roof.

   ○ sight ○ touch ○ hearing

2. The postcard from Colorado showed tall, rugged, snowcapped mountains.

   ○ touch ○ sight ○ smell

3. The scent of cinnamon floated in the air while the cookies baked.

   ○ sight ○ taste ○ smell

4. Jody snuggled her thick, fleece blanket as she fell asleep.

   ○ touch ○ sight ○ hearing

5. Janey made a funny face when she bit into the sour pickle.

   ○ taste ○ touch ○ hearing

6. The children watched the large, puffy clouds forming shapes in the sky.

   ○ hearing ○ sight ○ smell

7. The wind howled through the cracks in the old farmhouse.

   ○ sight ○ hearing ○ touch

8. "Ouch!" Sarah yelled when she stepped on the prickly thistle with her bare foot.

   ○ touch ○ sight ○ hearing

Mathematics

In the Mathematics chapter of this workbook, you will be practicing different types of problem-solving skills. Some of the worksheets will ask you to read a short paragraph and answer some questions relating to it. At times, you will need to refer to illustrations, graphs, or tables to find the information needed to complete the questions you are asked. You might be asked to show how you got your answer by solving the math problems inside a boxed area.

You will fill in a circle to respond to multiple-choice questions, write a word phrase or complete a sentence for short-answer questions.

Use this Mathematics Checklist to help you carefully complete your workbook pages.

Mathematics Checklist

- ☐ I read the problem information carefully.
- ☐ I underlined keywords or phrases to help me understand the story problems.
- ☐ I read the directions carefully and understood what I was supposed to do.
- ☐ I followed the directions that were given.
- ☐ I completed all the problems on the page.
- ☐ I checked my work.

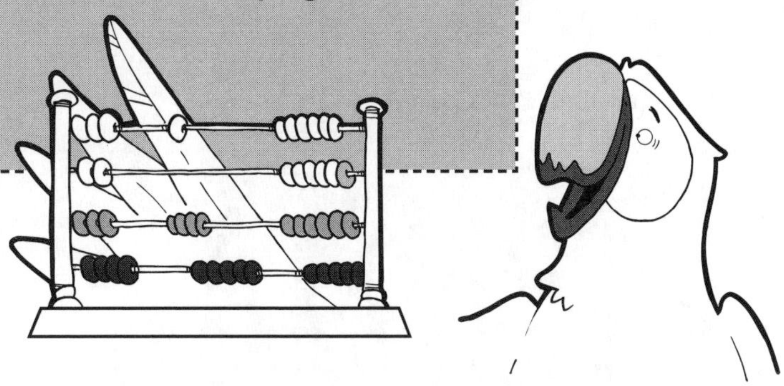

Directions: Solve the problems, then draw a line from the number phrase in Column A to its equivalent number phrase in column B. The first one has been done for you.

Column A	Column B
4 + 4 + 4 = 12	5 x 2 = ______
6 + 6 + 6 + 6 = ______	7 x 7 = ______
5 + 5 = ______	6 x 8 = ______
6 + 6 + 3 = ______	8 x 3 = ______
20 + 20 + 8 = ______	6 x 5 = ______
20 + 5 = ______	9 x 2 = ______
10 + 10 + 10 = ______	3 x 4 = 12
5 + 27 = ______	9 x 6 = ______
7 + 8 + 3 = ______	4 x 8 = ______
9+9+9+9+9+9 = ______	5 x 5 = ______
11 + 38 = ______	5 x 3 = ______

Directions: Use a completely filled circle to choose the answer choice that has the same value as each of the following whole numbers.

1. **461**

- ◯ 400 + 6 + 1
- ◯ 4 x 61
- ◯ four hundred sixty-one

2. **25**

- ◯ 5 + 5 + 5
- ◯ 5 x 5
- ◯ thirty-five

3. **333**

- ◯ 300 + 30 + 3
- ◯ three hundred thirty
- ◯ 33 + 3

4. **75**

- ◯ 70 x 5
- ◯ 70 – 5
- ◯ 7 tens + 5 ones

5. **2016**

- ◯ two thousand sixteen
- ◯ 2000 + 100 + 16
- ◯ two hundred sixteen

6. **654**

- ◯ 600 + 40 + 5
- ◯ 6 hundreds + 5 tens + 4 ones
- ◯ six hundred fifty

Directions: Use a completely filled circle to identify the symbol that correctly shows the comparison between the shaded areas of the shapes.

		>	=	<	
a.	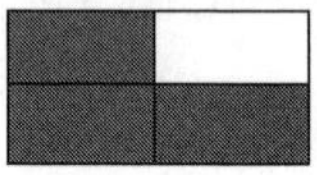	○	○	○	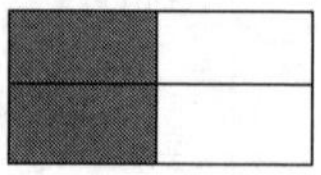
b.	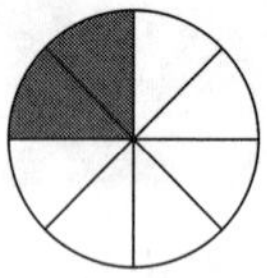	○	○	○	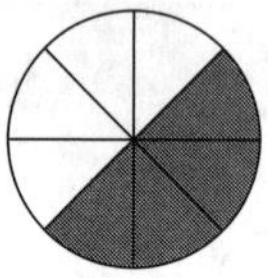
c.		○	○	○	
d.		○	○	○	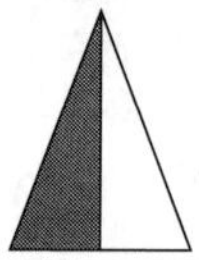

Directions: Use a completely filled circle to compare the following fractions.

		>	=	<	
e.	$\frac{1}{2}$	○	○	○	$\frac{1}{4}$
f.	$\frac{1}{3}$	○	○	○	$\frac{2}{3}$
g.	$\frac{1}{2}$	○	○	○	$\frac{2}{4}$
h.	$\frac{3}{8}$	○	○	○	$\frac{1}{2}$

Directions: Use a completely filled circle to compare the whole numbers and fractions in the left column to the whole numbers and fractions in the right column.

	>	=	<	
716	○	○	○	617
2,002	○	○	○	2,020
$\frac{1}{4}$	○	○	○	$\frac{1}{3}$
$\frac{1}{2}$	○	○	○	$\frac{2}{2}$
4,827	○	○	○	400 + 827
300 + 29	○	○	○	329
1	○	○	○	$\frac{1}{1}$
$\frac{1}{2}$	○	○	○	$\frac{1}{4}$
840 – 40	○	○	○	744
3,478	○	○	○	4,478 – 1000

Directions: David's class is learning how to write simple fractions as decimals. The teacher used a chocolate bar with 10 equal sections to show the students how equal fraction parts and decimals are written. One section of the chocolate bar is one out of ten (1 out of 10), or $\frac{1}{10}$, or 0.10. Use the picture of the chocolate bar to help you fill in the missing information in the table. The first one has been done for you.

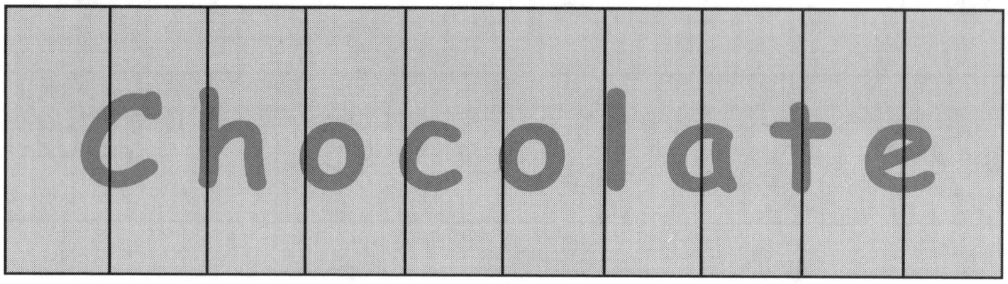

Written Words	Fraction	Decimal
one out of ten	$\frac{1}{10}$	0.10
six out of ten		
eight out of ten		
five out of ten		
three out of ten		
nine out of ten		
two out of ten		
seven out of ten		

Directions: Match the addition problem in the left column to the multiplication problem it equals in the right column. (Hint: How many times is the same number repeated in the addition column?) The first one has been done for you.

a. 2 + 2 + 2 + 2 + 2 + 2 + 2 + 2 + 2	8 x 2
b. 5 + 5 + 5 + 5 + 5	1 x 7
c. 8 + 8	3 x 6
d. 1 + 1 + 1 + 1 + 1 + 1 + 1	10 x 4
e. 4 + 4 + 4 + 4 + 4 + 4 + 4 + 4	2 x 9
f. 10 + 10 + 10 + 10	5 x 5
g. 3 + 3 + 3 + 3 + 3 + 3	9 x 5
h. 7 + 7 + 7 + 7 + 7 + 7	4 x 8
i. 6 + 6 + 6 + 6 + 6 + 6 + 6 + 6 + 6 + 6	7 x 6
j. 9 + 9 + 9 + 9 + 9	6 x 10

Directions: James invited three friends to his house for dinner. The boys shared an extra-large pepperoni pizza. Use the pizza illustration to help you answer the four questions.

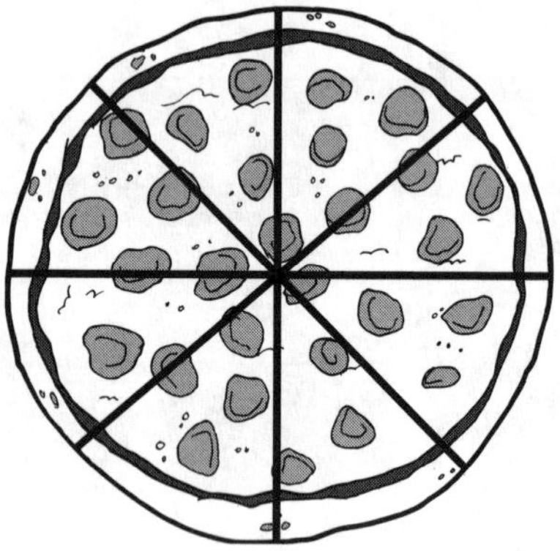

1. Douglas ate 3 slices of pizza. What fraction of the pizza did Douglas eat?

○ $\frac{1}{3}$

○ $\frac{3}{8}$

○ $\frac{1}{2}$

2. Tony ate the least. Which fraction represents the smallest amount of pizza?

○ $\frac{1}{2}$

○ $\frac{1}{3}$

○ $\frac{1}{8}$

3. Mario and James ate 2 slices each. What fraction of the pizza did they eat altogether?

○ $\frac{4}{3}$

○ $\frac{4}{8}$

○ $\frac{6}{8}$

4. Which fraction represents the whole pizza?

○ $\frac{7}{8}$

○ $\frac{8}{8}$

○ $\frac{1}{8}$

Directions: The boxes below show equations that follow the Commutative Law for addition and multiplication. Look at the equations in the left column. Write the matching equation on the line using the correct formula.

Commutative Law for Addition: a + b = b + a

Commutative Law for Multiplication: a x b = b x a

	Commutative Law
a. 140 + 60 =	______________________
b. 3 x 5	______________________
c. 20 x 6	______________________
d. 337 + 221	______________________
e. 10 x 10	______________________
f. 589 + 146	______________________

Solve one of the equations to prove the Commutative Law.

______________________ = ______________________

Answer = ______________

Directions: The boxes below show equations that follow the Associative Law for addition and multiplication. Look at the equations in the left column. Write the matching equation on the line using the correct formula.

Associative Law for Addition: $a + (b + c) = (a + b) + c$

Associative Law for Multiplication: $a \times (b \times c) = (a \times b) \times c$

Associative Law

a. $12 + (33 + 40) =$ ______________________

b. $3 \times (1 \times 2) =$ ______________________

c. $(27 + 14) + 23 =$ ______________________

d. $6 \times (4 \times 3) =$ ______________________

e. $(10 \times 1) \times 10 =$ ______________________

f. $74 + (12 + 6) =$ ______________________

Solve one of the equations to prove the Associative Law.

______________________ = ______________________

Answer = ______________

Directions: Read the sentences in the left column. Select the correct measuring units needed to measure in each situation. Use a completely filled circle to mark your answer choice.

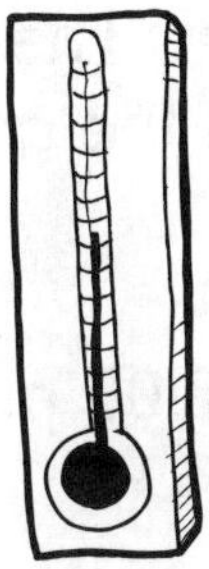

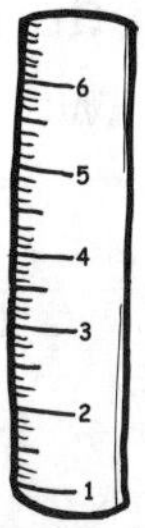

	degrees	cups, quarts, and gallons	feet, miles, meters, and kilometers	ounces, pounds, and grams
1. Jessie is finding out the exact number of quarts in six gallons.	○	○	○	○
2. Riley swims the length of the pool four times every day.	○	○	○	○
3. The bag of dog food weighs as much as Blake's dog.	○	○	○	○
4. Gina is comparing the temperatures outside and inside.	○	○	○	○
5. Paige measured the height of her plant.	○	○	○	○
6. The candy bar and the six pebbles weigh the same.	○	○	○	○

Directions: Read the statement about elapsed time carefully. Use a completely filled circle to show the time that correctly answers each question. Use the boxes on the right to show your work.

1. The baseball game started at 1:00 p.m. The game lasted two hours. What time did the game end?

   ◯ 1:00 p.m. ◯ 2:00 p.m. ◯ 3:00 p.m.

2. Teresa leaves for school at 8:30 a.m. She gets up one hour before she leaves. What time does Teresa get up in the morning?

   ◯ 7:30 a.m. ◯ 8:30 a.m. ◯ 9:30 a.m.

3. Gerald is going to the park after school. It takes 15 minutes to get to the park. School lets out at 3:15 p.m. What time will Gerald arrive at the park?

   ◯ 3:15 p.m. ◯ 3:30 p.m. ◯ 3:45 p.m.

4. Mara went to the beach at 11:00 a.m. She stayed there for one and a half hours. What time did she leave the beach?

   ◯ 11:30 a.m. ◯ 12:00 noon ◯ 12:30 p.m.

Directions: Read each of the thermometers shown below. Write the correct temperature in degrees Fahrenheit (ºF) or degrees Celsius (ºC) on the line provided.

1.

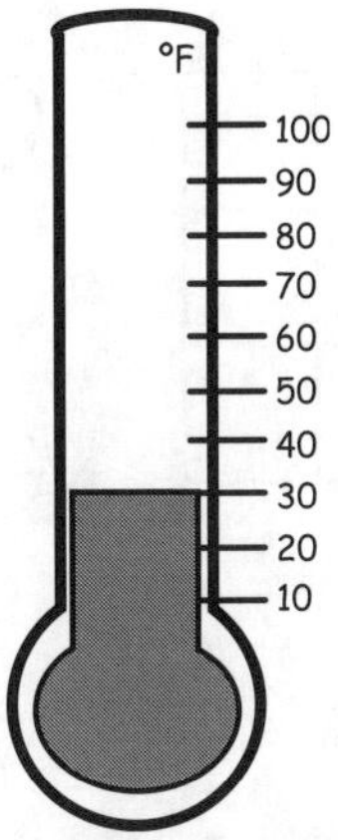

____

2.

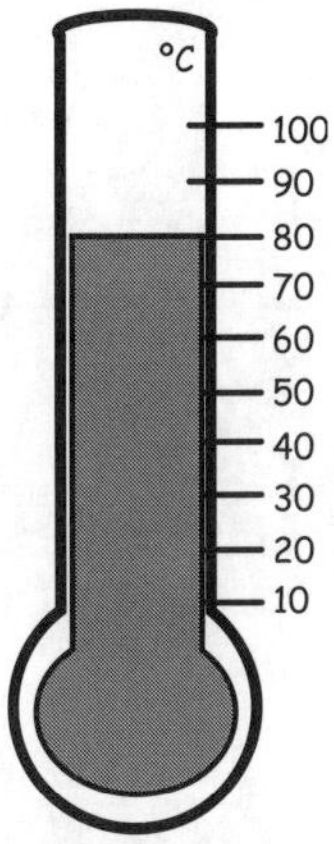

____

3.

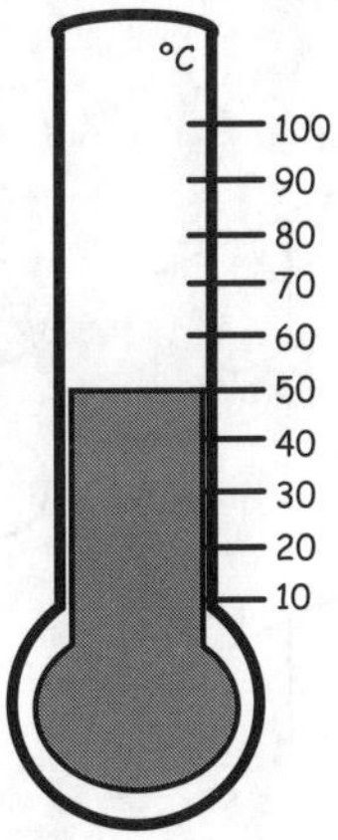

____

4.

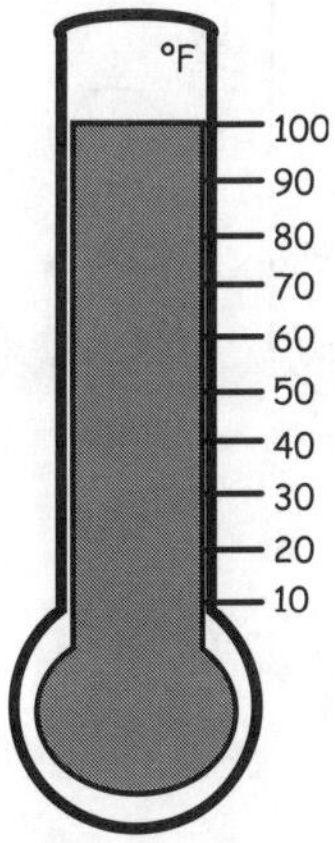

____

5.

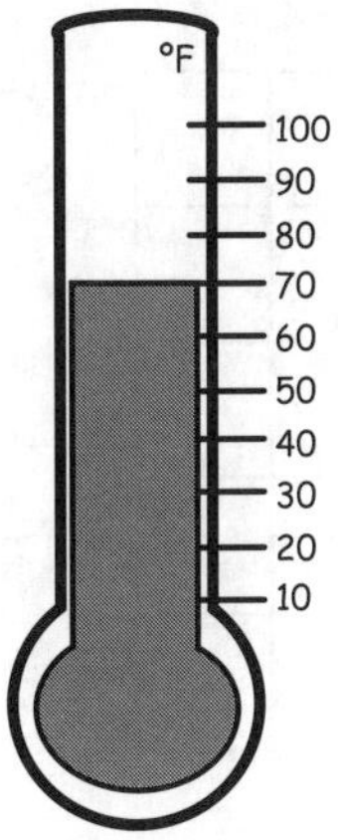

____

6.

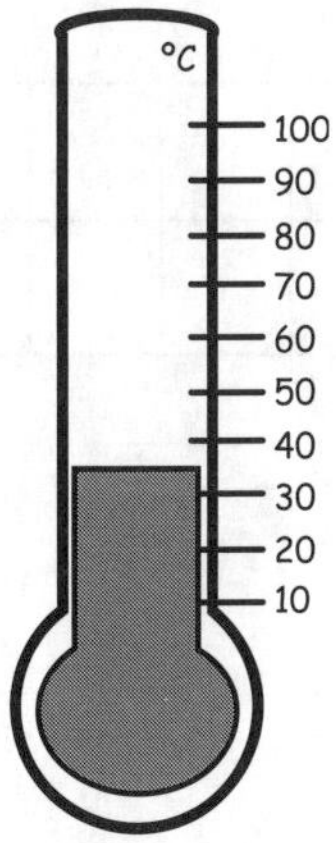

____

Directions: Find the number of units in the area of the figures pictured. Use a completely filled circle to mark your answer choice.

A.

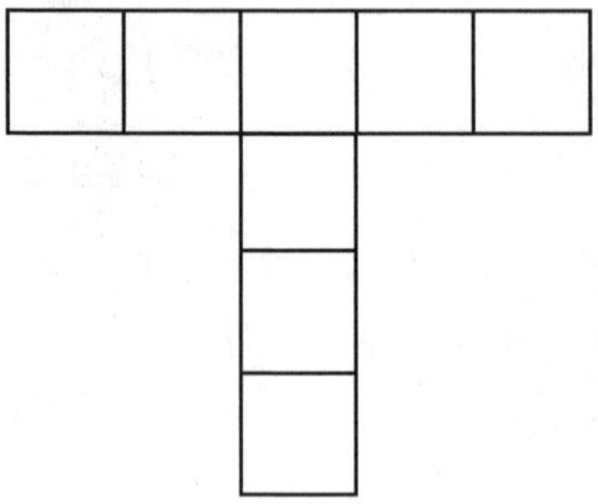

○ 9

○ 6

○ 8

B.

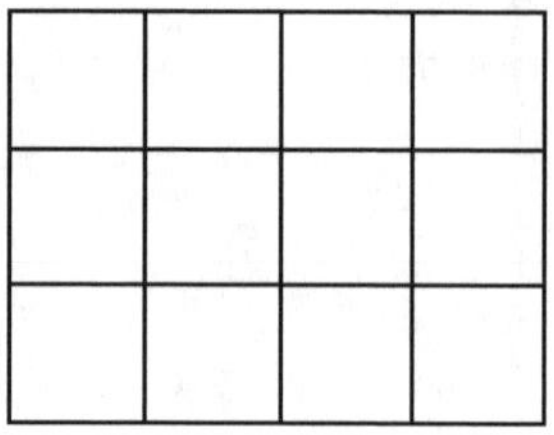

○ 12

○ 14

○ 16

C.

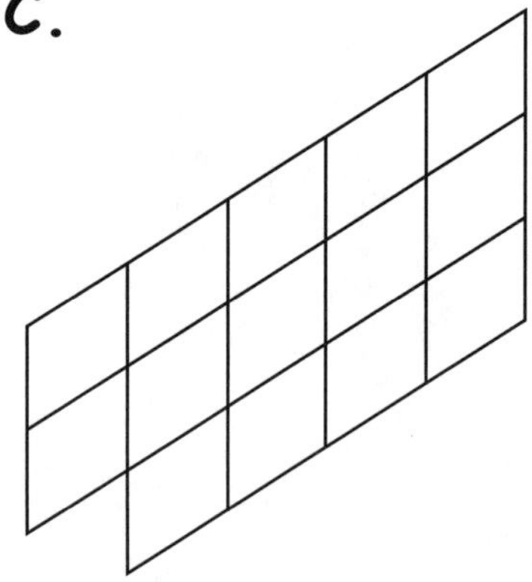

○ 15

○ 14

○ 16

D.

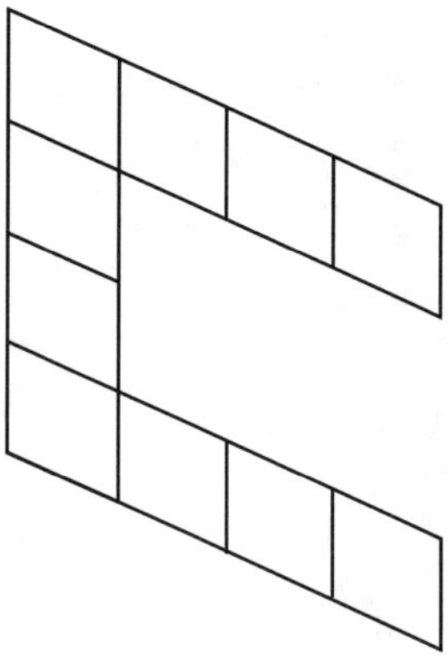

○ 10

○ 11

○ 12

E.

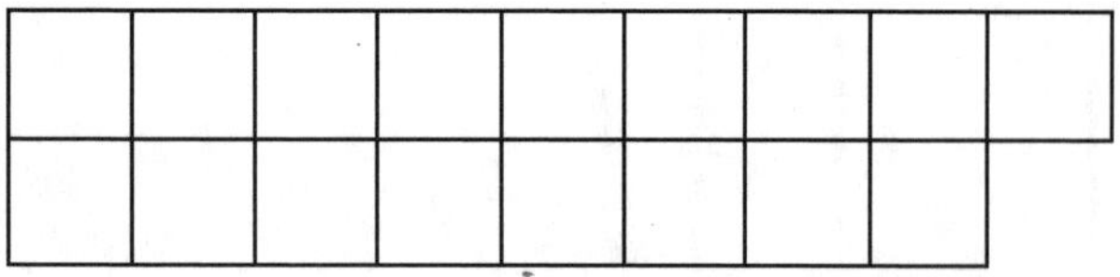

17	19	20
○	○	○

F.

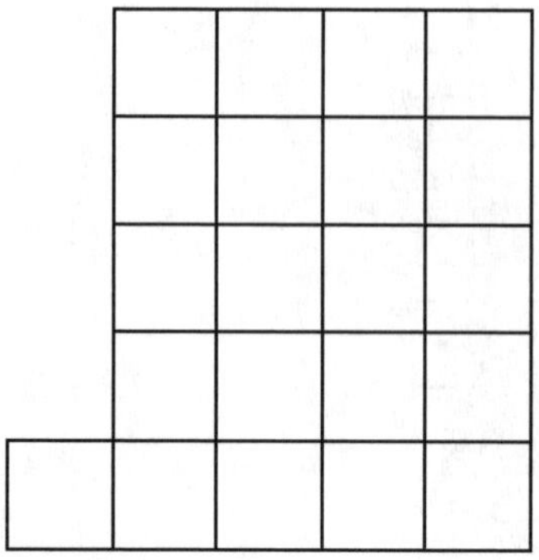

○ 19

○ 21

○ 25

Directions: Look at the six geometric figures below. Use a completely filled circle to answer each question about them.

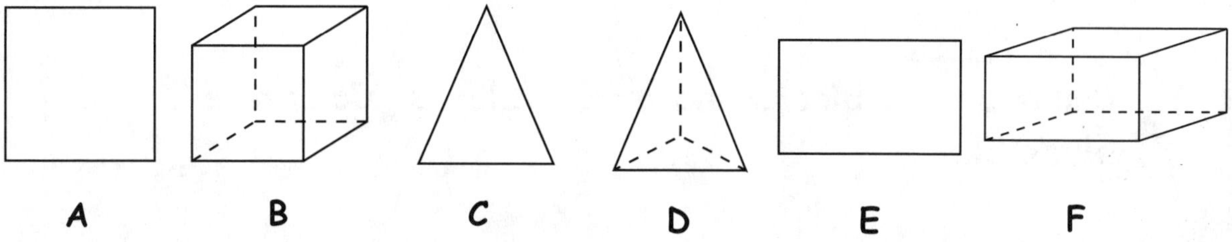

1. Which of the above figures are two-dimensional?
   - ◯ A, B, F
   - ◯ A, C, E
   - ◯ A, C, F

2. Which of the above figures are three-dimensional?
   - ◯ B, D, F
   - ◯ B, D, E
   - ◯ B, C, F

3. How many faces do figures A and C each have?
   - ◯ 1
   - ◯ 2
   - ◯ 3

4. How many sides do figures A and E each have?
   - ◯ 4
   - ◯ 5
   - ◯ 6

5. How many faces does figure D have?
   - ◯ 3
   - ◯ 4
   - ◯ 6

6. How many faces does figure B have?
   - ◯ 4
   - ◯ 6
   - ◯ 8

Directions: Read each set of directions. Find and color the correct block on the grid on page 85. Use the star as your starting point for each set of directions.

1. Count over → 6 blocks and up ↑ 5 blocks. Color the block blue.

2. Count over → 2 blocks, up ↑ 3 blocks, and over → 1 block. Color the block yellow.

3. Count up ↑ 7 blocks, over → 4 blocks, and up ↑ 1 block. Color the block red.

4. Count up ↑ 3 blocks and over → 8 blocks. Color the block orange.

5. Count over → 4 blocks, up ↑ 4 blocks, and over → 4 blocks. Color the block green.

6. Count up ↑ 5 blocks, over → 3 blocks, and up ↑ 1 block. Color the block purple.

7. Count up ↑ 2 blocks, over → 2 blocks, up ↑ 3 blocks, and over → 1 block. Color the block brown.

Directions: Follow the directions from page 84 to color the correct blocks on the grid below. Use the star as your starting point each time for each set of directions.

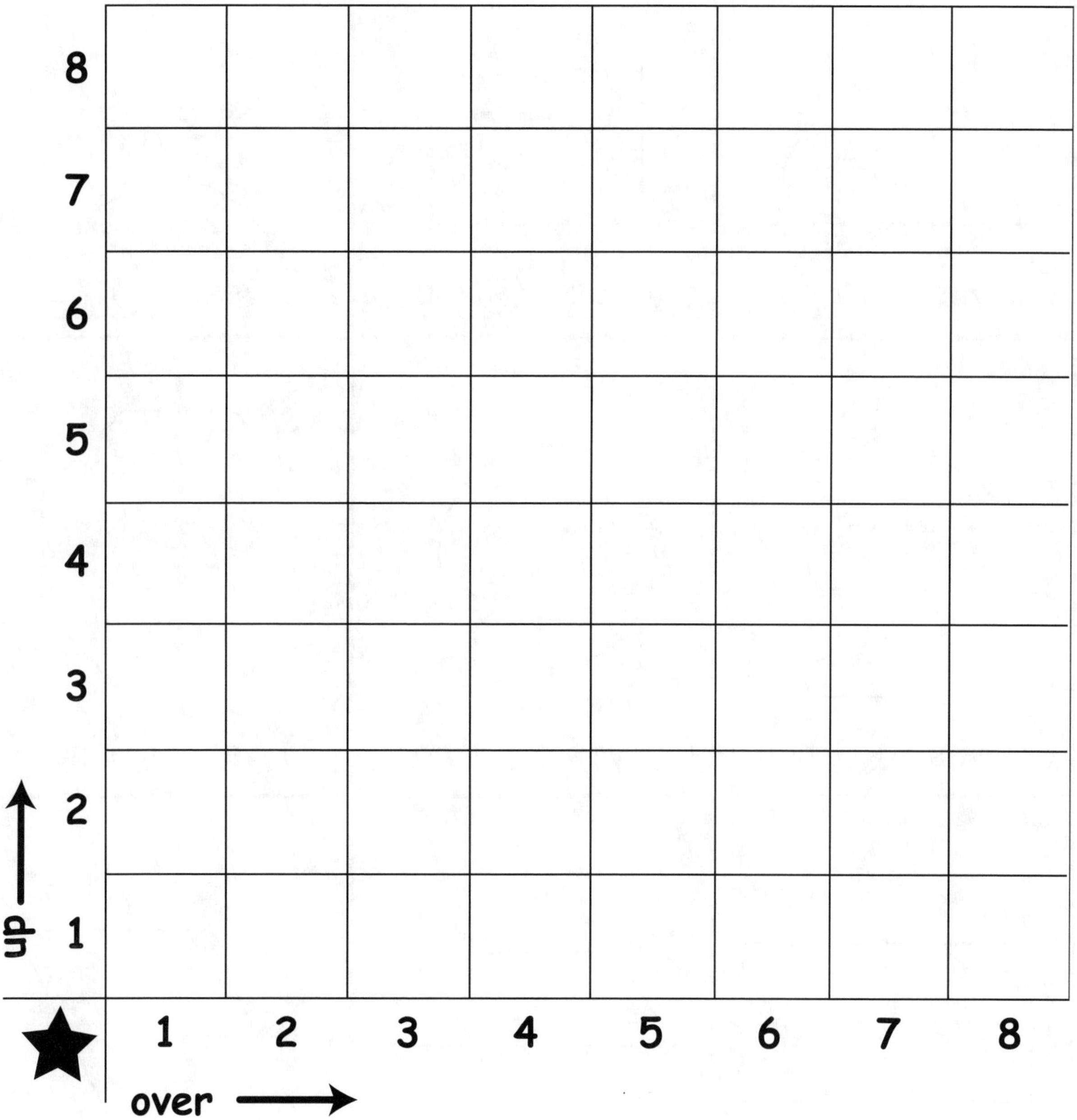

Directions: Look at the figure in each box. Each figure has a dotted line drawn through it. If the figure is folded on the dotted line, will the two halves match? Use a completely filled circle to show whether each figure is symmetrical. The first one has been done for you.

1.

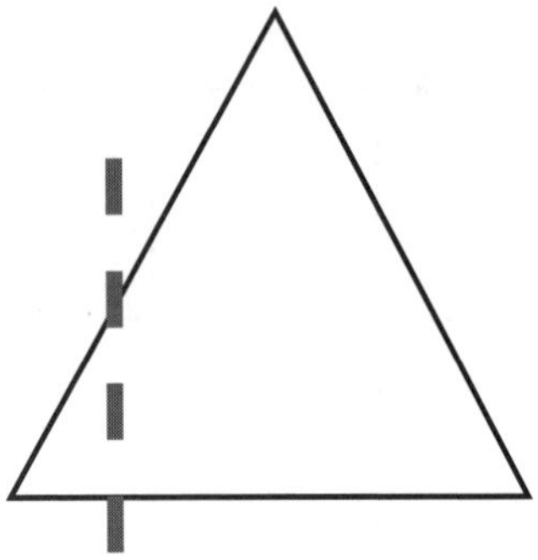

○ yes ● no

2.

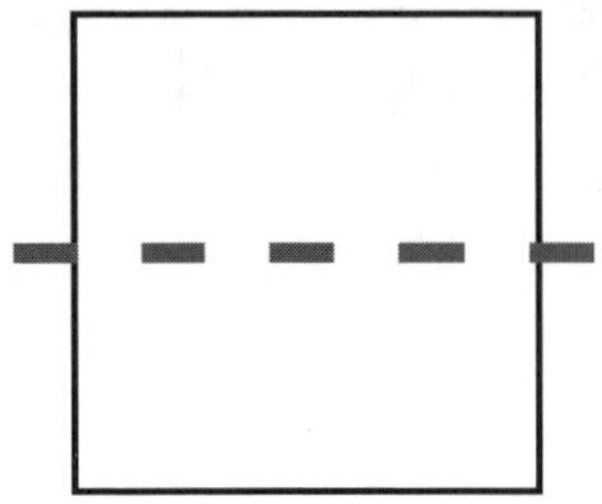

○ yes ○ no

3.

○ yes ○ no

4.

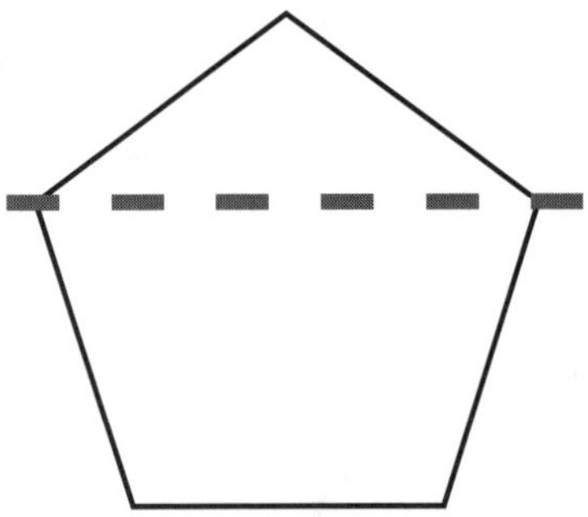

○ yes ○ no

5.

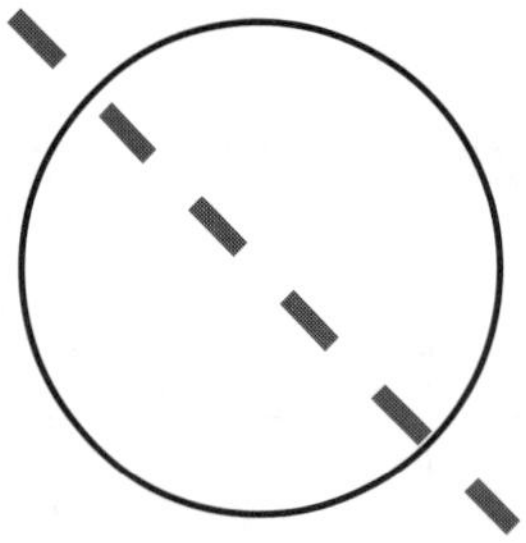

○ yes ○ no

6.

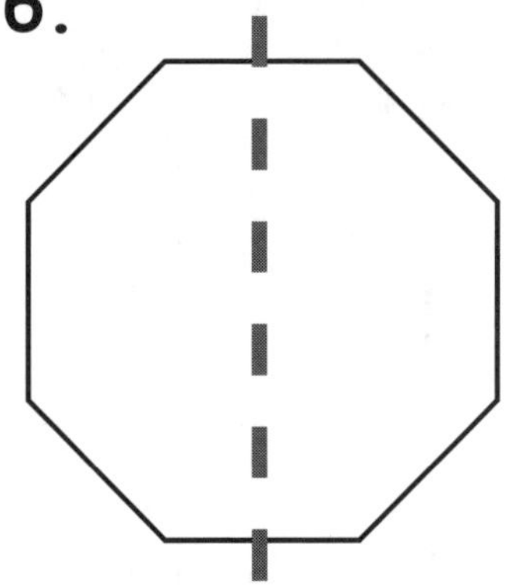

○ yes ○ no

7.

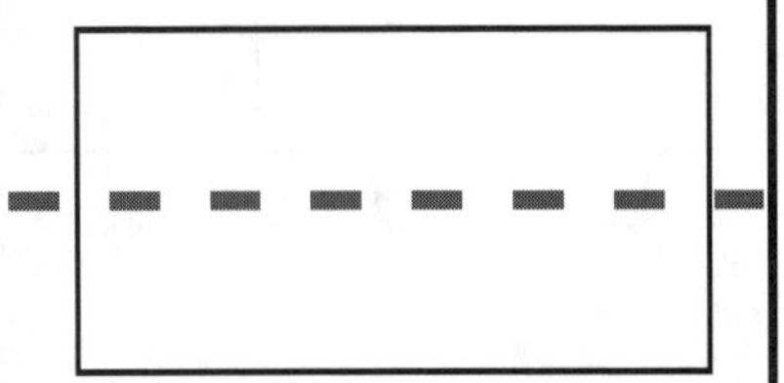

○ yes ○ no

8.

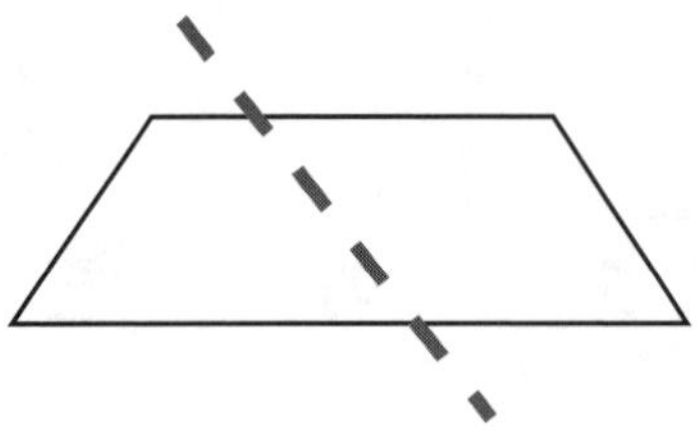

○ yes ○ no

9.

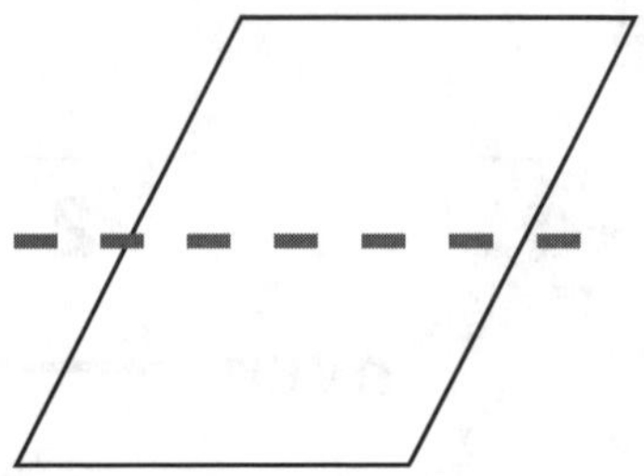

○ yes ○ no

Directions: Write the number on the blank line that correctly completes each sequence. Draw a line to match each sequence to the correct rule. The first one has been done for you.

a. 10, 15, 20, 25	The rule is to subtract 10.
b. ______, 57, 54, 51	The rule is to multiply by 3.
c. 27, 9, ______	The rule is to add 2.
d. 12, 14, ______, 18	The rule is to add 5.
e. 2, 4, ______, 16	The rule is to subtract 5.
f. 90, ______, 70, 60	The rule is to multiply by 2.
g. 1, 3, ______, 27	The rule is to divide by 3.
h. 75, 70, 65, ______	The rule is to subtract 3.

Directions: Fill in the blank with the number that completes each of the following patterns.

a. ______, 40, 60, ______, 100, 120, ______, 160

b. $1.00, $1.25, ______, $1.75, $2.00, ______, ______

c. 97, 84, 71, 58, ______, 32, ______, ______

d. $\frac{7}{7}$, ______, $\frac{5}{7}$, $\frac{4}{7}$, ______, $\frac{2}{7}$, ______

e. 0.04, 0.08, ______, 0.16, 0.20, ______, 0.28, ______

f. 1,300, 1,100, ______, 700, ______, 300, ______

g. 2, 4, 8, ______, 32, ______, 128, ______

h. 100%, ______, 90%, 85%, ______, 75%, ______

Directions: Choose the piece that correctly completes each pattern. Use a completely filled circle to mark your answer choice.

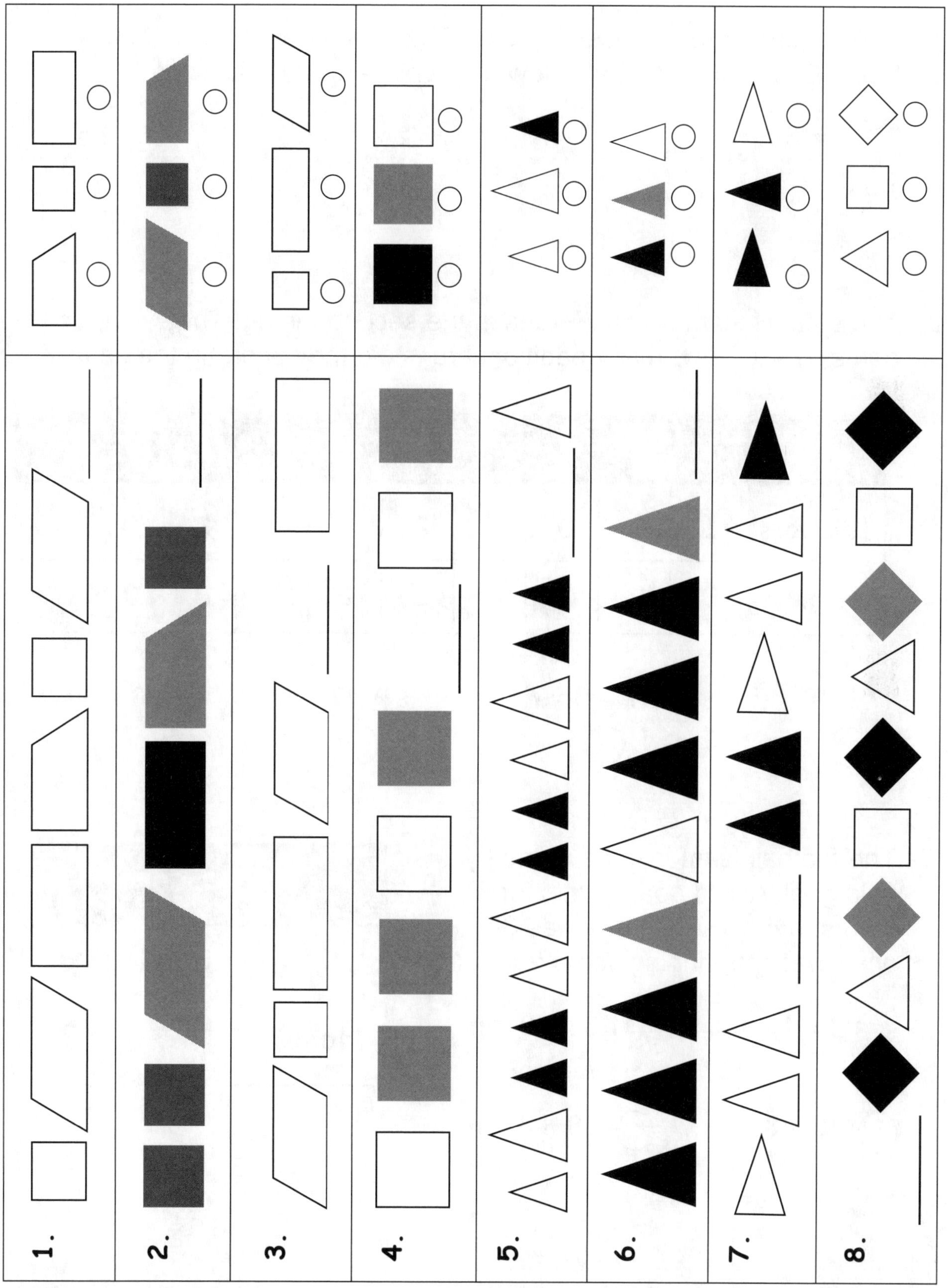

Directions: Read each problem carefully. Select the equation that solves the problem correctly. Use a completely filled circle to mark your answer choice.

1. The soccer team practices in pairs. The coach gave 7 balls to the team. Each pair got 1 ball. How many players are practicing?

$7 + 2 = \mathbf{n}$	$7 - 2 = \mathbf{n}$	$2 \times 7 = \mathbf{n}$	$7 \div 2 = \mathbf{n}$
○	○	○	○

2. The softball team scored 9 runs in the second inning. They won the game 17–10. How many additional runs did they score in the game?

	1	2	3	4	5	6	7	8	9	F
Visitors	1	0	0	3	2	1	1	2	0	10
Home	0	9	2	0	1	1	4	0	0	17

$17 - 10 = \mathbf{n}$	$17 - 9 = \mathbf{n}$	$9 + 17 = \mathbf{n}$	$10 - 9 = \mathbf{n}$
○	○	○	○

3. The football team lost the game by 1 field goal. A field goal counts for 3 points. If the losing score was 38, what was the winning score?

Final Score	
Visitors	38
Home	?

○ $3 \times 1 = \mathbf{n}$ ○ $38 \div 3 = \mathbf{n}$

○ $38 - 3 = \mathbf{n}$ ○ $38 + 3 = \mathbf{n}$

Directions: A number is missing in each of the problems below. The letter **n** is used to show that a number is missing. Find the missing number for each problem. Use a completely filled circle to mark your answer choice. The first one has been done for you.

1. 17 + **n** = 19	● 2	○ 3	○ 4
2. 23 + 23 = **n**	○ 44	○ 46	○ 64
3. 44 – 11 = **n**	○ 23	○ 33	○ 43
4. 88 – **n** = 44	○ 35	○ 41	○ 44
5. 12 + 44 = **n**	○ 36	○ 46	○ 56
6. **n** + 10 = 95	○ 15	○ 75	○ 85
7. 58 – **n** = 37	○ 21	○ 12	○ 32
8. 117 – 16 = **n**	○ 109	○ 101	○ 121

Directions: A number is missing in each of the multiplication problems below. The letter **n** is used to show that a number is missing. Find the missing number for each problem. Use a completely filled circle to mark your answer choice. The first one has been done for you.

1. 4 x **n** = 4	● 1	○ 2	○ 3
2. **n** x 2 = 6	○ 1	○ 2	○ 3
3. 2 x 2 = **n**	○ 3	○ 4	○ 5
4. 3 x **n** = 9	○ 3	○ 4	○ 5
5. **n** x 2 = 10	○ 4	○ 5	○ 6
6. 4 x 1 = **n**	○ 4	○ 5	○ 6
7. 3 x **n** = 12	○ 3	○ 4	○ 5
8. 5 x **n** = 15	○ 3	○ 4	○ 5

Directions: Use the number table below to complete items 1 and 2.

3	10		24	
	17	24		
		31		45
24	31			
	38	45		59

1. Write the rule for completing the number table.

____

____

2. Complete the number table by filling in the blank squares with the correct numbers.

Directions: Use the table below to complete items 3 through 6.

A	B
3	9
1	
4	12
2	
	15
	30
6	18

3. Write the rule for completing the number table.

____

4. Complete the table on the left. Fill in the missing numbers.

5. What are the missing numbers in Column A?

○ 7, 10
○ 5, 24
○ 5, 10

6. What are the missing numbers in Column B?

○ 7, 6
○ 3, 6
○ 3, 8

Directions: Look at the pictograph below to answer the six questions about it. Use a completely filled circle to mark your answer choice.

A Button Pictograph

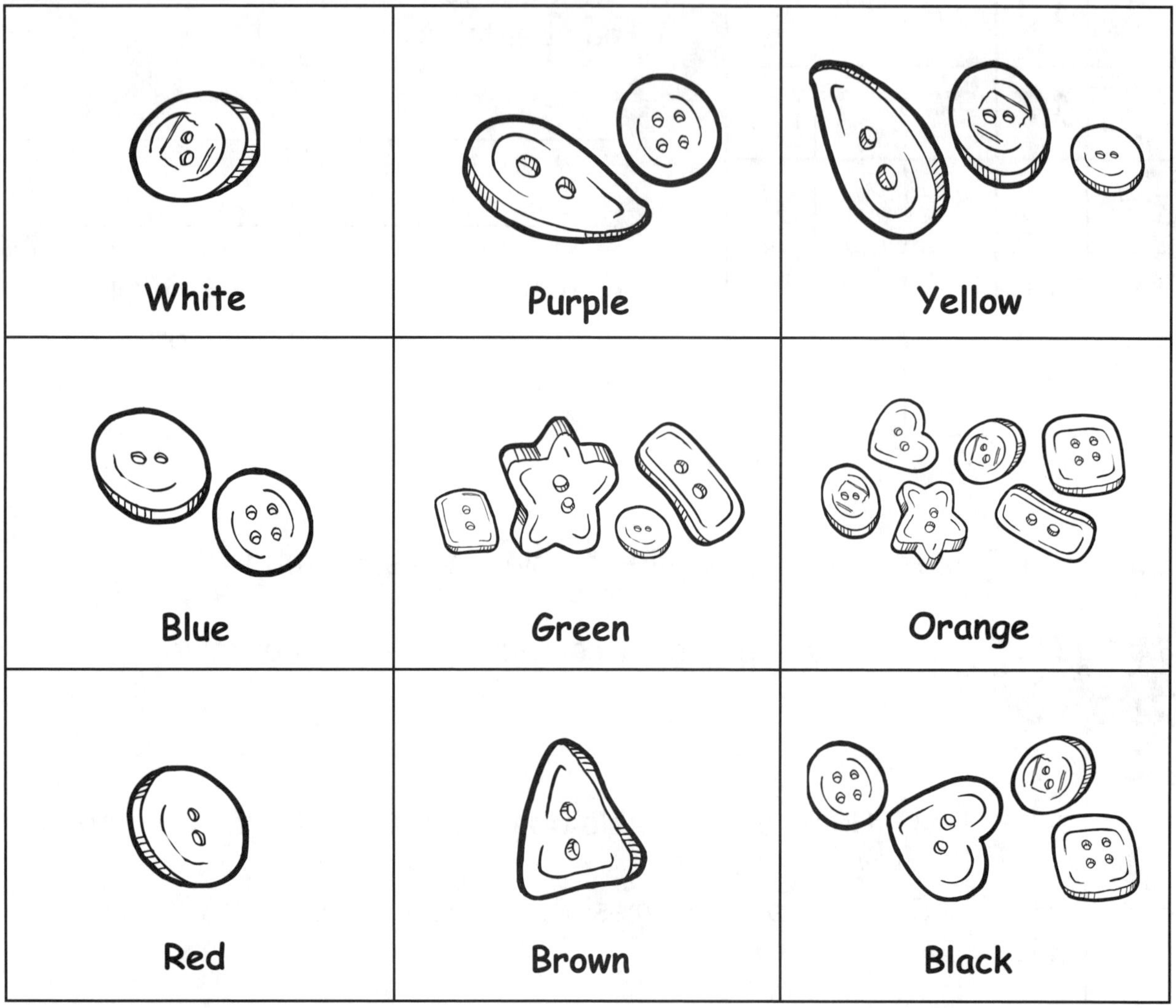

1. Which number represents the total number of buttons displayed on the pictograph?

   ○ 20 ○ 21 ○ 24 ○ 25

2. Which number represents the total number of color categories displayed on the pictograph?

   ○ 8 ○ 9 ○ 10 ○ 12

3. Which fraction shows the number of buttons with only 2 holes displayed in the pictograph?

○ $\frac{18}{24}$ ○ $\frac{19}{20}$ ○ $\frac{19}{24}$ ○ $\frac{18}{25}$

4. Which fraction shows the number of buttons with 4 holes displayed in the pictograph?

○ $\frac{16}{22}$ ○ $\frac{5}{24}$ ○ $\frac{4}{22}$ ○ $\frac{6}{24}$

5. Which fraction shows the number of white, green, and orange buttons displayed in the pictograph?

○ $\frac{10}{22}$ ○ $\frac{12}{24}$ ○ $\frac{11}{22}$ ○ $\frac{11}{24}$

6. Each color represents a fraction of the total number of buttons. What is the common denominator of all the fractions?

○ 20 ○ 22 ○ 24 ○ 25

Numerator = the top number in a fraction

Denominator = the bottom number in a fraction

Directions: Read the following information and use it to make a graph. (Hint: Underline important information to help you draw the correct number of columns for your graph.)

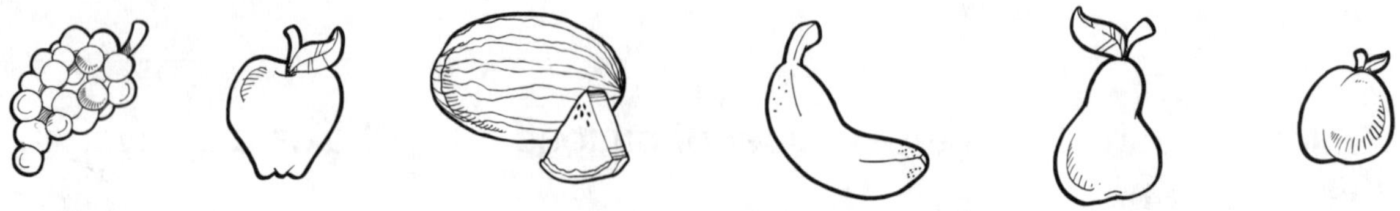

The class decided to make a fruit salad. Each member of the class had to bring one type of fruit. Five students brought bananas. Julie and Jim each contributed a watermelon. Marcy, Jen, William, Kim, and Ray brought apples. Peaches were given by seven children. Two students contributed pears, while the rest of them provided grapes.

Create a bar graph that illustrates the fruits these 25 students combined for their fruit salad.

Title ______________________________

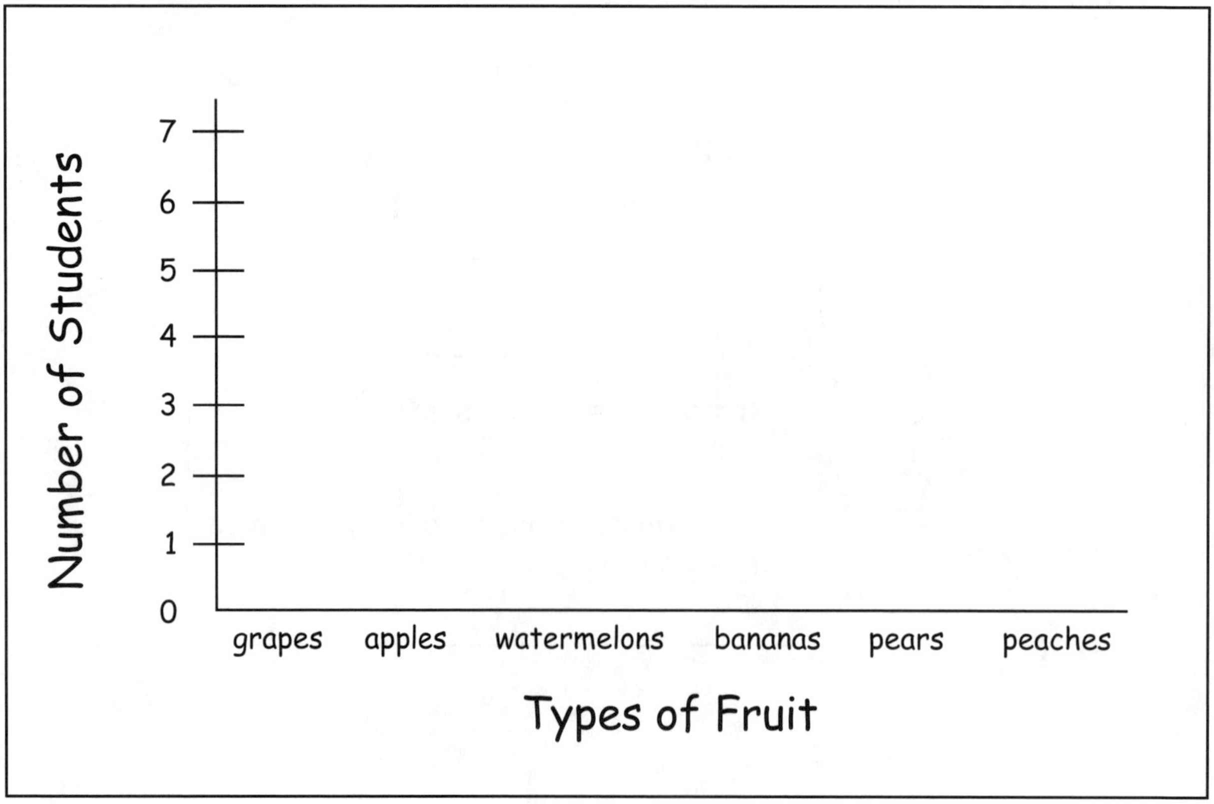

Directions: The following data was collected during a one-week period. The cafeteria manager kept track of the lunch count for 50 students in third grade to see which lunches they bought most often. Use a completely filled circle to answer the four questions about the lunch data.

	Monday	Tuesday	Wednesday	Thursday	Friday
Weekly Lunch Menu	peanut butter and jelly sandwich	chicken nuggets	2 tacos	grilled cheese	pepperoni or cheese pizza
Lunch Count	18	19	25	18	40

1. Which number shows the range of the data?

   ◯ 21 ◯ 22 ◯ 15 ◯ 5

2. Which number shows the mode of the data?

   ◯ 18 ◯ 19 ◯ 25 ◯ 40

3. Which number shows the mean (average) number of lunches bought during the week?

   ◯ 18 ◯ 19 ◯ 24 ◯ 25

4. Select the fraction that shows how many students bought lunch on the day the most students bought lunch.

   ◯ $\frac{1}{2}$ ◯ $\frac{9}{25}$ ◯ $\frac{1}{4}$ ◯ $\frac{4}{5}$

range = the difference between the largest and the smallest number
mean = the average of all the numbers given
median = the middle number when the numbers are arranged from lowest to highest
mode = the number that occurs the most often

Directions: The students in the third-grade classrooms are planning their end-of-the-year pizza party. During the school year, they learned how to take polls, gather data, and understand the information they collected. The students are using these skills to order pizza for everyone to eat. All of the third graders were asked what kind of pizza they liked best. Then, the students displayed their data on a circle graph.

Look at the circle graph below. Use the information on it to answer the four questions about it. Use a completely filled circle to mark your answer choice.

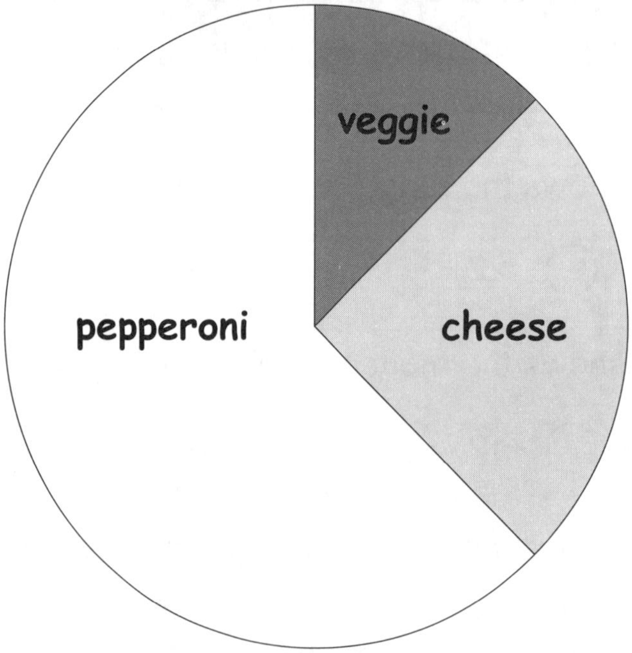

	Yes	No
1. Does the circle graph show the kind of pizza that the most students chose?	○	○
2. Does the circle graph show the kind of pizza that the fewest students chose?	○	○
3. Does the circle graph show the exact number of pizzas that need to be ordered?	○	○
4. Does this graph show the number of students used in the data collection?	○	○

Directions: The students in Mr. O'Malley's third-grade class decided to take a poll to find out their favorite subjects. Use the information from the chart below to create a bar graph display of the data that has been collected. Be sure to label the *x*-axis and the *y*-axis and add a title.

Favorite Subjects Poll

Subjects	Number of Students
Writing	𝍸 |
Reading	𝍸 ||
Math	||||
Citizenship	|||
Science	𝍸

Directions: Every Thursday, the classes at Sunshine Elementary School return their books to the school library. The librarian keeps a chart showing the number of books returned by each grade, from kindergarten (K) to sixth (6). Look at the chart below and answer the five questions about it.

K	20
1	40
2	25
3	40
4	40
5	25
6	30

1. What number appears most often in this chart?

   ◯ 25 ◯ 30 ◯ 40

2. What is the largest number in this chart?

   ◯ 25 ◯ 30 ◯ 40

3. What is the smallest number in this chart?

   ◯ 20 ◯ 25 ◯ 30

4. Write the mode (the number that appears most often) on the line below.

   ____

5. Subtract the smallest number in the chart from the largest number in the chart to find the range of this data. Write this number sentence (equation) in the box below.

Directions: A poll was conducted among the students in the third-grade classes to find out what kind of hard candy each student liked best. Every third-grade student voted for his or her favorite flavor of hard candy. The results of the students' votes are shown in the pictograph.

Study the data. Use it to answer the four questions below. Use a completely filled circle to mark your answer choice.

In one bag of candies, there are 10 strawberry candies, 10 orange candies, and 10 lemon candies.

	Yes	No
1. Will there be enough candies in one bag for each student who likes orange to get one piece of orange candy?	○	○
2. The students who like the candy with the fewest number of votes each want two pieces of candy. Are there enough candies of that flavor in one bag?	○	○
3. Will everyone who likes strawberry candies best be able to get a strawberry piece from one bag?	○	○

4. How many bags of candy would you need for every student who likes strawberry best to get one piece of strawberry candy?

   ○ two ○ three ○ four

Directions: Simon wants to organize his weekly activities. When he completes an activity, he puts a check in the box. Use Simon's chart to help you answer the four questions about his weekly activities. Use a completely filled circle to mark your answer choice.

	Sunday	Monday	Tuesday	Wednesday	Thursday	Friday	Saturday
Feed the dog	✓	✓	✓	✓	✓	✓	✓
Take out the trash			✓				
Ball games		✓			✓		✓
Library volunteer			✓			✓	
Music lesson				✓			

1. What activity does Simon do on 3 out of 7 days?
   - ◯ library volunteer
   - ◯ music lesson
   - ◯ ball games
   - ◯ take out the trash

2. Which combination of activities occurs on 5 out of 7 days?
   - ◯ take out the trash and music lesson
   - ◯ library volunteer and take out the trash
   - ◯ music lesson and ball games
   - ◯ ball games and library volunteer

3. What activity does Simon do on 7 out of 7 days?
   - ◯ feed the dog
   - ◯ take out the trash
   - ◯ ball games
   - ◯ library volunteer

4. On which day does Simon have the most activities?
   - ◯ Monday
   - ◯ Tuesday
   - ◯ Wednesday
   - ◯ Thursday

Social Studies

The Social Studies chapter of this workbook will help you practice skills related to the benchmarks that the state of Ohio has designated for third grade. You will be asked to use different types of information to determine your answer choices. There will be some short reading passages that will have questions for you to answer about the information that you read. You will also be asked to use a variety of tables, maps, and illustrations to answer some questions.

You will be responding to three different kinds of questions. A filled circle will be used for multiple-choice answers. Write a word, a phrase, or a complete sentence for a short-answer question, and write more sentences with supporting details for an extended-response question.

Use this Social Studies Checklist to help you review the information you were asked to complete on your workbook pages.

Social Studies Checklist

- ☐ I read the information on the page carefully.
- ☐ I followed directions that were given.
- ☐ I used the tables, maps, or graphs to help me understand and answer the questions.
- ☐ I filled in circles or wrote complete answers to the questions I was asked.
- ☐ I answered all the questions on the page.
- ☐ I checked my answers carefully.

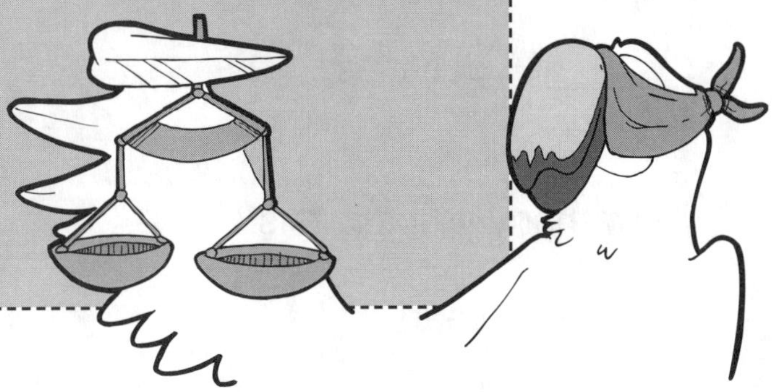

Directions: Read each of the following statements carefully. Answer the questions by writing the correct number on the line. (Hint: Use what you know about years, decades, and centuries to help you.)

1. The museum docent told the students that the painting is from 1802.

   How many centuries ago was the picture painted?

   ________ centuries

2. Dane's grandparents celebrated their 50th wedding anniversary.

   How many decades have his grandparents been married?

   ________ decades

3. Cailee will be a teenager on her next birthday.

   How can she show her age in decades and years?

   ________ decade(s)   ________ years

4. Ohio celebrated its bicentennial of statehood in 2003.

   How many centuries is this?

   ________ centuries

   How many decades is this?

   ________ decades

   How many years is this?

   ________ years

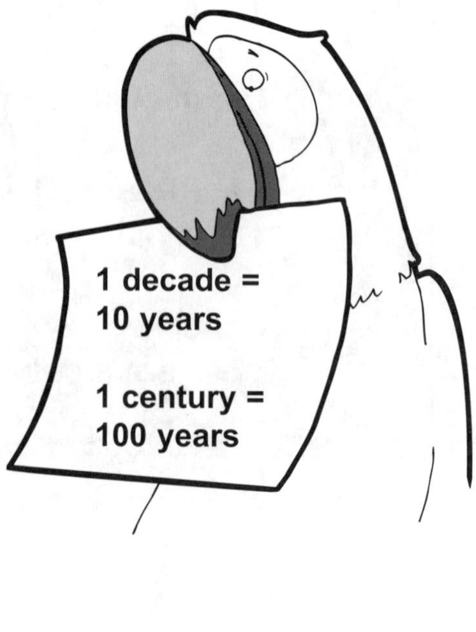

Directions: Place the names of Ohio's state symbols on the timeline according to the year they were adopted by the state legislature.

buckeye tree

1933
cardinal

1902
flag

1975
ladybug

1988
white-tailed deer

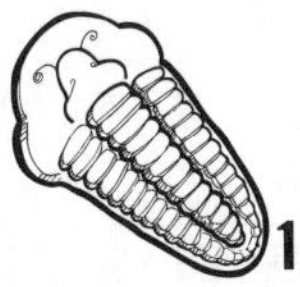
1985
trilobyte (official state fossil)

1900
1910
1920
1930
1940
1950
1960
1970
1980
1990
2000

Directions: Ryan's class is studying some of the different ways that towns and communities can grow and change. Ryan's great-grandmother still lives in the same community where she grew up. Ryan decided to personally ask Grandma Tess about the changes she has seen.

Read Ryan's interview with Grandma Tess, then answer the questions that relate to it. Use a completely filled circle to mark your answer choice.

Ryan: "How long have you lived here?"

Grandma Tess: "I was born in this house eighty-seven years ago."

Ryan: "How has the land changed since you were my age?"

Grandma Tess: "When I was your age, this house was surrounded by farmland. Now, my house is inside the town with other houses, buildings, and businesses around it."

Ryan: "What happened to your farmland?"

Grandma Tess: "As the community began to grow with new businesses, the farmland was sold to make room for new houses and buildings. People bought the houses because there were jobs here and they could work."

1. How has the town where Grandma Tess lives changed since she was a child?

   ○ There's more farmland. ○ There's less farmland. ○ There's no change.

2. Why did people move into Grandma Tess's town?

   ○ There were jobs. ○ There were parks. ○ There were houses.

3. Why is Grandma Tess's house inside the town now?

   ○ The house was moved. ○ The house was sold. ○ The town's area grew larger.

Directions: Several students in Mrs. King's third-grade class were discussing cultural traditions that their families celebrate during the year. Draw a line to identify which cultural group is most likely to celebrate each tradition.

1. Zachary's family and neighbors work together to build barns throughout the community.
2. Jackson's family celebrates Kwanzaa.
3. Mary and her brother break piñatas at parties.
4. Kathleen wears a green sweater on St. Patrick's Day.
5. Kim's parents taught him how to eat with chopsticks.
6. George's grandfather says, "Gesundheit," when George sneezes.
7. Amy participates in tribal dancing with her family.

Directions: Use the political map of Ohio's counties to answer the questions about it. Use a completely filled circle to mark your answer choice.

A **political map** shows features of the Earth on a flat surface (e.g., boundaries, capitals, political areas, etc.).

1. What county is farthest south?

   ○ Scioto ○ Gallia ○ Lawrence

2. What county is farthest north?

   ○ Ashtabula ○ Lake ○ Lucas

3. What county is east of Licking County?

   ○ Knox ○ Coshocton ○ Fairfield

4. What county is west of Clinton County?

   ○ Warren ○ Fayette ○ Highland

Directions: Look at the physical map of Wildwoods Park to answer the questions about it. Use a completely filled circle to mark your answer choice.

A **physical map** shows landforms, elevations, and other physical features of the Earth on a flat surface.

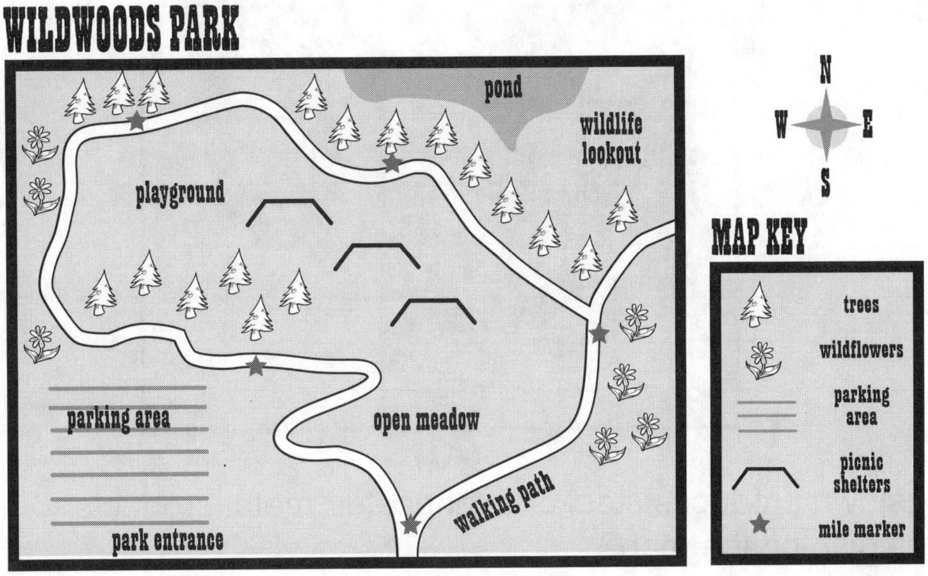

1. Where is the playground located in the park?

   ◯ northwest ◯ northeast ◯ southwest

2. How long is the walking path?

   ◯ 5 miles ◯ 6 miles ◯ 7 miles

3. Which landform is located near the Wildlife Lookout?

   ◯ playground ◯ meadow ◯ pond

4. What is found on the east side and west side of Wildwoods Park?

   ◯ wildflowers ◯ pond ◯ meadow

Directions: The grid map below identifies certain cities in Ohio. Read the sentences about the products these cities make. Use a completely filled circle to find the city that is described.

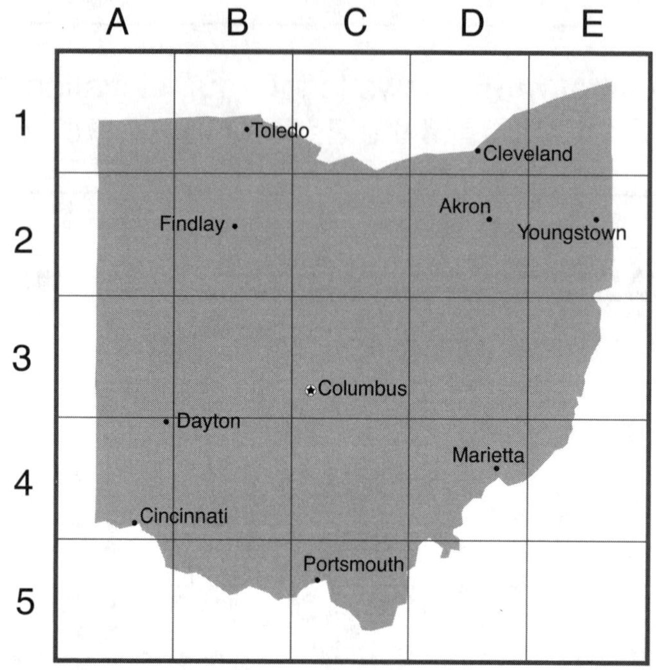

1. Youngstown produces steel and fabricated metal products. Where is Youngstown on the map?

   ○ 1E ○ 2D ○ 2E

2. Columbus has the only metal whistle factory in the nation. Where is Columbus on the map?

   ○ 4A ○ 3C ○ 5C

3. Rubber, plastics, and food products are made in Findlay, Ohio. Find it on the map.

   ○ 1B ○ 2B ○ 3B

4. Cars and industrial machinery are produced in Dayton. Where is Dayton on the map?

   ○ 3B ○ 4A ○ 4B

Directions: Look at the diagram below to help you answer the questions about it. Write complete sentences for your responses.

1. How has the environment changed?

____

____

____

2. How has the community changed?

____

____

____

3. List three ways that the community can be helpful to the environment.

a. ____

b. ____

c. ____

Directions: People, products, and ideas move from place to place on a daily basis. Read the sentences below and decide the best means for transporting each. Use a completely filled circle to mark your answer choice.

1. The family is driving to the Grand Canyon for a vacation.

   ◯ airplane ◯ automobile ◯ fax machine

2. Fruits and vegetables are delivered to the local markets.

   ◯ truck ◯ telephone ◯ taxi

3. Max's dad flies to California for a business meeting on Tuesday.

   ◯ fax machine ◯ automobile ◯ airplane

4. Shani calls her friend about a homework assignment.

   ◯ bus ◯ telephone ◯ truck

5. The class is going on a field trip to the city park.

   ◯ airplane ◯ bus ◯ telephone

6. Steel cargo is going from the east coast to the west coast.

   ◯ train ◯ car ◯ telephone

7. The secretary sent the contract to the customer immediately.

   ◯ boat ◯ train ◯ fax machine

8. Oil is transported from the Middle East to another part of the world.

   ◯ automobile ◯ airplane ◯ cargo ships

Directions: Read the following passage that shows an example of opportunity cost (the value of another choice when a decision is made). Answer the two questions that follow using complete sentences for your responses.

Sergio likes playing the guitar. He has been taking lessons for two years. Sergio's music teacher feels that he has a special talent. The music teacher suggested that Sergio increase his lessons from once a week to twice a week.

1. If Sergio decides to take an extra guitar lesson each week, what is something he can gain?

____

____

____

____

____

2. If Sergio decides to take an extra guitar lesson each week, what is something he will give up?

____

____

____

____

____

Directions: Read each of the sentences in the left column carefully. Decide whether a production or a consumption activity is being described. Use a completely filled circle to mark your answer choice.

	production	consumption
1. Anna is mixing lemonade for the booth at the carnival.	○	○
2. The author wrote a new chapter book.	○	○
3. Betsy used a ticket for the train ride.	○	○
4. Roland planted tomatoes, beans, carrots, and peppers in the garden.	○	○
5. Dede bought cookies at the bake sale.	○	○
6. The carpenter painted the table for his store.	○	○
7. Robert spent $1.00 at the garage sale.	○	○
8. Sally needed to buy new school supplies.	○	○

Directions: Read the following phrases to see whether goods (products) or services are being described. Use a completely filled circle to mark your answer choice.

	goods	services
1. brownies at the bake sale	○	○
2. mowing Mr. Brown's grass	○	○
3. a new pair of shoes	○	○
4. balloons at the carnival	○	○
5. librarian reading a story	○	○
6. babysitting your brother	○	○
7. a docent at the zoo	○	○
8. pencils in the supply cart	○	○
9. apples in the cafeteria	○	○
10. walking the neighbor's dog	○	○
11. fresh fruit from the orchard	○	○
12. driving the school bus	○	○

Directions: Every year the students in third grade are invited to be "City Officials for a Day." The children take a bus downtown to the administration building where the government offices are located. They will follow the city officials during a workday to see how the local government helps the community and the citizens.

The students used the building directory to help them find the city officials they would follow. On the next page, use a completely filled circle to show which floor the students will find the city official they are following for the day.

Administration Building Directory	
1st Floor	Mayor City Attorney City Planner City Council President
2nd Floor	Chief of Police Street Superindendent Clerk of Courts
3rd Floor	Auditor Building Inspector Parks and Recreation Director

1. Shannon, Mark, Kelsey, and Lacey are working with the person who inpects buildings for safety.

   ◯ 1st floor ◯ 2nd floor ◯ 3rd floor

2. Damien, Brady, Marla, and Katie will meet with the person in charge of the city.

   ◯ 1st floor ◯ 2nd floor ◯ 3rd floor

3. Ramon, Ashley, Scott, and Missy are learning about taking care of the city's parks.

   ◯ 1st floor ◯ 2nd floor ◯ 3rd floor

4. Michael, Kevin, Maria, and Lisa are finding out how the police department works.

   ◯ 1st floor ◯ 2nd floor ◯ 3rd floor

5. Explain why local government offices are usually located in the downtown area of towns and cities.

   ____

   ____

   ____

   ____

   ____

Directions: Read each of the following passages carefully. Write one or two sentences to describe how the community benefits.

1. Maria's parents help to plan the city's annual art festival. How does this help the community?

____

____

____

2. Before every election, Carl learns about the local issues and the people running for political office. He votes in every election. How does Carl help the community?

____

____

____

3. Yoko's family has a restaurant in the town. How does this help their community?

____

____

____

4. Tyler's grandmother volunteers at his elementary school. How is she helping the community?

____

____

____

Directions: For the past ten years, the third graders at Franklin Elementary School have hosted a neighborhood pet show. During the first planning session for this year's show, students discovered that three of their classmates were allergic to long animal fur. The class organized a group meeting to talk about the annual pet show.

Use this information to help you respond to the items below. Write your answers in complete sentences.

1. The students are having a group meeting to discuss the pet show. What situation do they need to talk about?

___

___

___

2. Brandon is in charge of the meeting. He will only let one person speak at a time. He wants to hear all points of view about the pet show. Is this a good way to conduct a meeting? Explain your answer.

___

___

___

3. Describe one way that all the students can participate in the pet show this year.

___

___

___

Directions: The school librarian is helping the students gather information for their Social Studies reports. The students are learning that the table of contents, title page, illustrations, and keyword searches can help them find information in a source.

Read each statement carefully. Decide which part of the source material the student needs to use, then use a completely filled circle to mark your answer choice.

1. Jared chose a topic, but he needs more resource information about it.

   ◯ Table of Contents ◯ Keyword search ◯ Illustrations

2. Rickie wants to use the September 2002 issue of *Wildlife Magazine*.

   ◯ Keyword search ◯ Illustrations ◯ Title page

3. Deena needs to find the chapter about the ancient tribes who inhabited the area.

   ◯ Illustrations ◯ Table of Contents ◯ Keyword search

4. Louis used the photographs to compare the city in 1956 and 2003.

   ◯ Table of contents ◯ Illustrations ◯ Title page

Directions: Each of the following sentences states a **cause** (something that happened). Write a sentence below each cause that shows an **effect** (something that results from the cause). The first one has been done for you.

1. Jenny's grandma bought two yards of fabric at the store.

   Jenny's grandma made her a new dress.

2. There was five inches of snow on the ground in the morning.

3. Maria planted beans and carrots in the garden.

4. The class decided to have a bake sale.

5. It was a very windy day.

Directions: A flow chart is a way to organize and display various kinds of information. Read the passage below about Raquel. Then, answer the four questions about Raquel's flow chart organizer on the next page.

Raquel used the flow chart below to organize her book collection. First, she divided her books into two categories: fiction and nonfiction. Next, she divided the fiction and nonfiction books into paperback and hardcover books. Then, Raquel placed the books on different colored shelves.

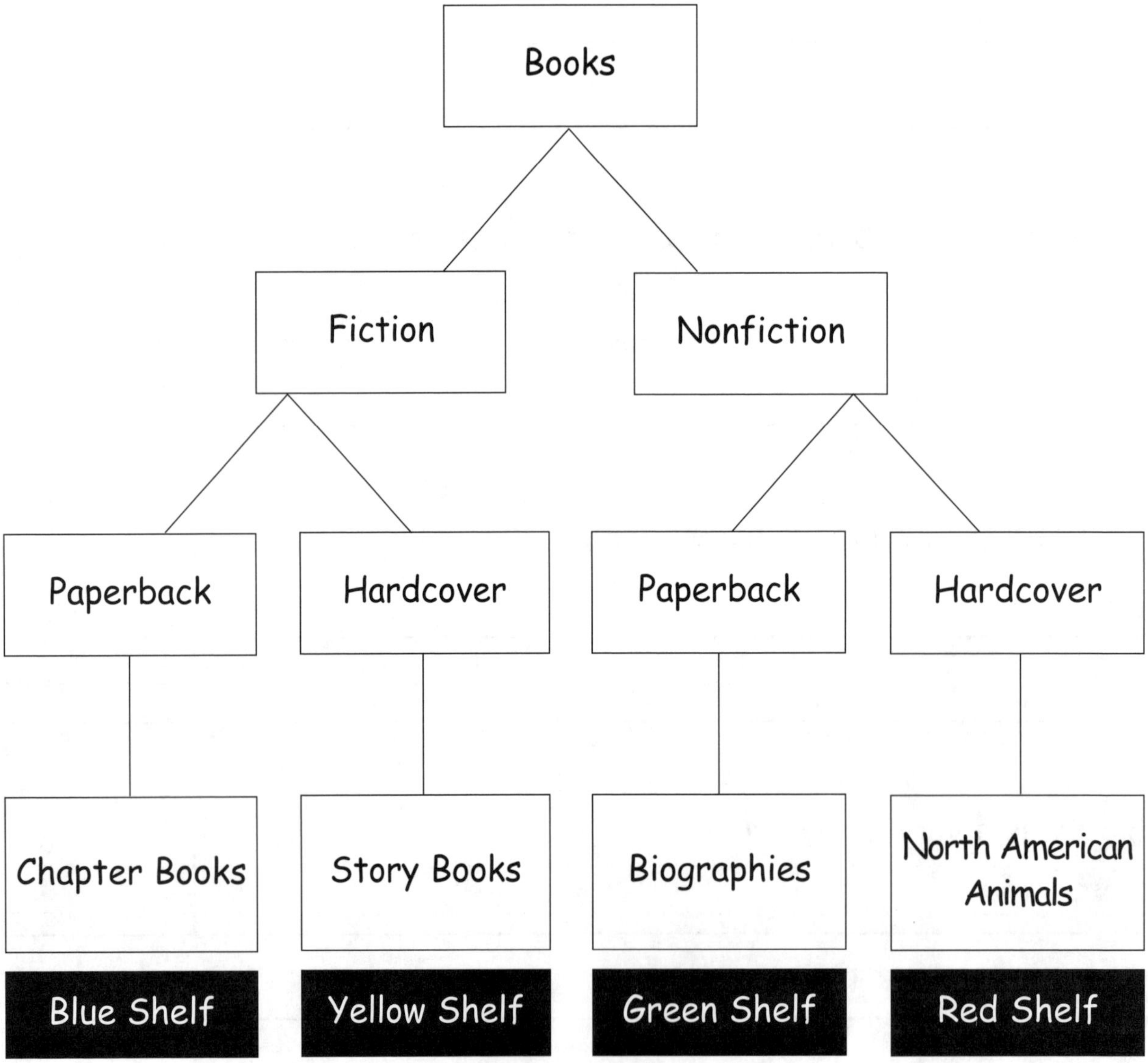

Directions: Refer to the passage about Raquel and Raquel's flow chart organizer on the previous page to answer the four questions below. Use a completely filled circle to mark your answer choice.

Where will Raquel find:

1. a biography about Abraham Lincoln?
   - ◯ blue shelf
   - ◯ green shelf
   - ◯ red shelf

2. a book about wild horses in the United States?
   - ◯ yellow shelf
   - ◯ blue shelf
   - ◯ red shelf

3. a paperback copy of *Charlotte's Web*?
   - ◯ blue shelf
   - ◯ yellow shelf
   - ◯ red shelf

4. her favorite fairy tales?
   - ◯ yellow shelf
   - ◯ blue shelf
   - ◯ green shelf

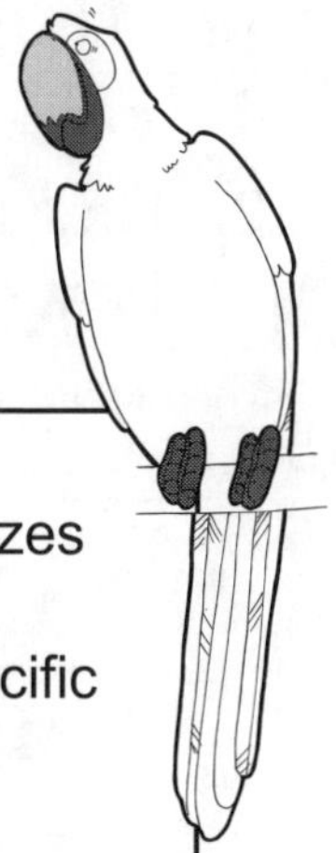

A **flow chart** organizes information from a general topic to specific topics.

Directions: Following a trip to the zoo, the students collected the data displayed on the bar graph below. Use the information from the graph to answer the questions about it. Write your answers in complete sentences.

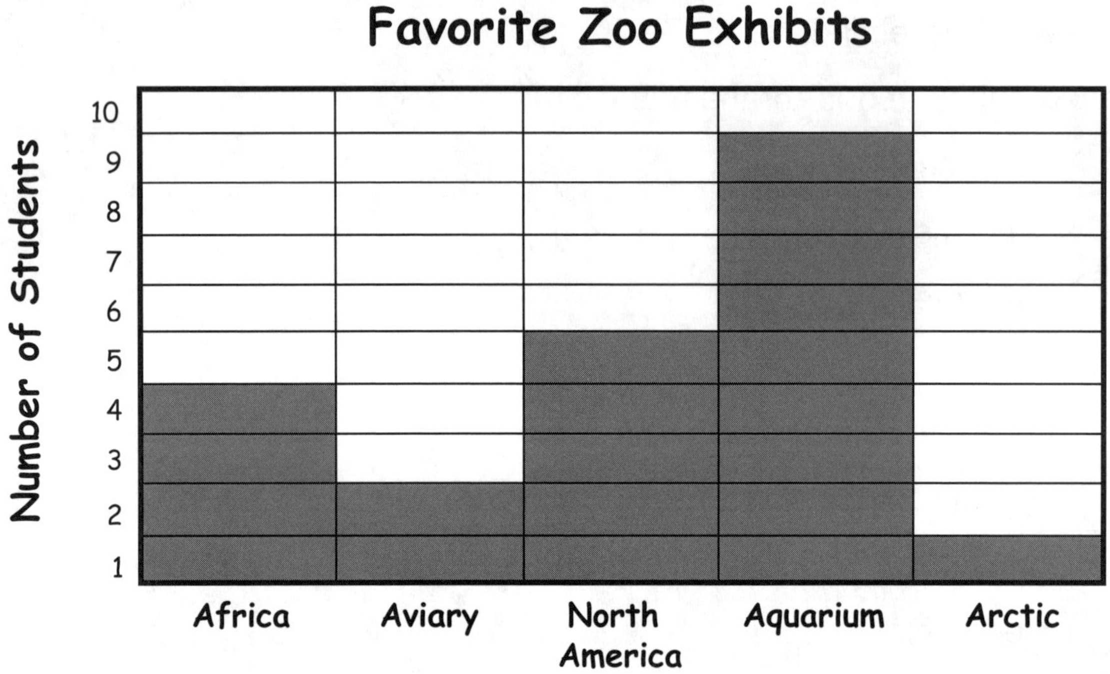

1. Which exhibit did the least number of students vote as their favorite?

____

____

____

2. How many students liked the African and North American exhibits best?

____

____

____

3. Use the graph information to state one fact about the students' favorite zoo exhibits.

4. List three different things that this graph tells you.

a.

b.

c.

5. Write your opinion (what you think) to explain why only one student chose the Arctic exhibit as the favorite.

Directions: Read the following passage carefully, then answer the questions that follow using phrases or complete sentences.

Last year, Mrs. Cole's third-grade class planted a wildflower garden in the back of the school. The garden is beautiful because this year's class is continuing to take care of it. Mrs. Cole was told that a new school addition is planned where the garden is now planted. When Mrs. Cole presented the building plans to the class, she suggested that they use the problem-solving and decision-making process to discuss it.

(Identifying the problem)

1. What is the problem the students will discuss?

____

____

____

(Gathering information)

2. What do the students need to know about the new building?

____

____

____

3. What do the students need to know about the wildflower garden?

(Listing and considering options)

4. What is one thing the students might do?

(Considering advantages and disadvantages of options)

5. What is one advantage of the new building?

6. What is one advantage of the wildflower garden?

7. What is one disadvantage of the new building?

____

____

____

8. What is one disadvantage of the wildflower garden?

____

____

____

(Choosing and implementing a solution)

9. In your opinion, what do you think could happen?

____

____

____

____

____

____

Science

The Science chapter of this workbook will help you practice answering many questions using different types of information. The questions will require you to fill in a circle to designate your answer for multiple-choice questions, write a word, a phrase, or a complete sentence for a short-answer question, or write more sentences with supporting details for an extended-response question.

You will be asked to read charts, tables, graphs, and simple keys, then use the information contained in them to answer certain questions. Use all the skills you have learned about collecting, interpreting, and evaluating scientific information to help you understand what you are being asked.

Use this Science Checklist to remind you to complete each workbook page carefully.

Science Checklist

- [ ] I read the information carefully.
- [ ] I used illustrations, graphs, or tables on the page to help me understand the information better.
- [ ] I followed the directions that were given.
- [ ] I responded appropriately by filling in a circle, writing a short answer, or writing more information with supporting details.
- [ ] I answered all the questions on the page.
- [ ] I checked my answers carefully and added more information when needed.

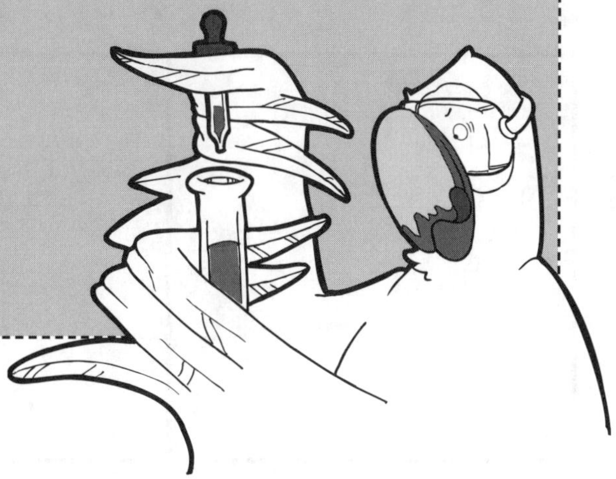

Directions: Read the information about Mark below. Use the information to complete the two activities.

Mark found his rock collection under his bed. These are the kinds of rocks he had in the box:

- A large, smooth, gray rock;
- A large, smooth, gray rock with sparkles in it;
- A large, brown rock with sharp edges;
- A large, black, shiny chunk with sharp edges; and
- Two small rocks, one with orange stripes and one solid colored.

1. Mark wants to organize his collection into a container that has three sections. List three properties of the rocks Mark might use to sort his collection.

   1. ______________________________

   2. ______________________________

   3. ______________________________

2. Create the categories you might use if you were sorting Mark's collection in the spaces below.

Directions: The third graders at King Avenue School are studying how smaller rocks are formed from larger rocks. Their teacher informed them that the process called physical weathering could be the result of the actions of plant growth, wind, or water. Use a completely filled circle to tell what you think caused the weathering of the rocks in the examples below.

1. The roots of the tree broke through the sidewalk.

   ○ plant growth ○ wind ○ water

2. The rocks and shells turned into sand on the Lake Erie beach.

   ○ plant growth ○ wind ○ water

3. The jagged edges on the granite sign were smoothed.

   ○ plant growth ○ wind ○ water

4. The oak tree grew in the crevice of the sandstone wall.

   ○ plant growth ○ wind ○ water

5. The continuous drip from the roof formed a dent in the rock below it.

   ○ plant growth ○ wind ○ water

6. There were small bits of sand at the base of the sandstone statue.

   ○ plant growth ○ wind ○ water

7. The powerful motion of the waves cut a ridge into the limestone wall.

   ○ plant growth ○ wind ○ water

8. The dandelion pushed its way up through the sidewalk.

   ○ plant growth ○ wind ○ water

Directions: Marcie and Gary were attending a soil workshop at the local park. The naturalist gave each of the children a cup of soil and asked them to make a list of the things they found in the soil. Their lists are given below. Use the lists to complete the missing information on the Venn diagram.

Marcie's List	Gary's List
worm	walnut shell
dead leaves	ant
grass	tree roots
seeds	dead leaves
beetle	rocks
rocks	button

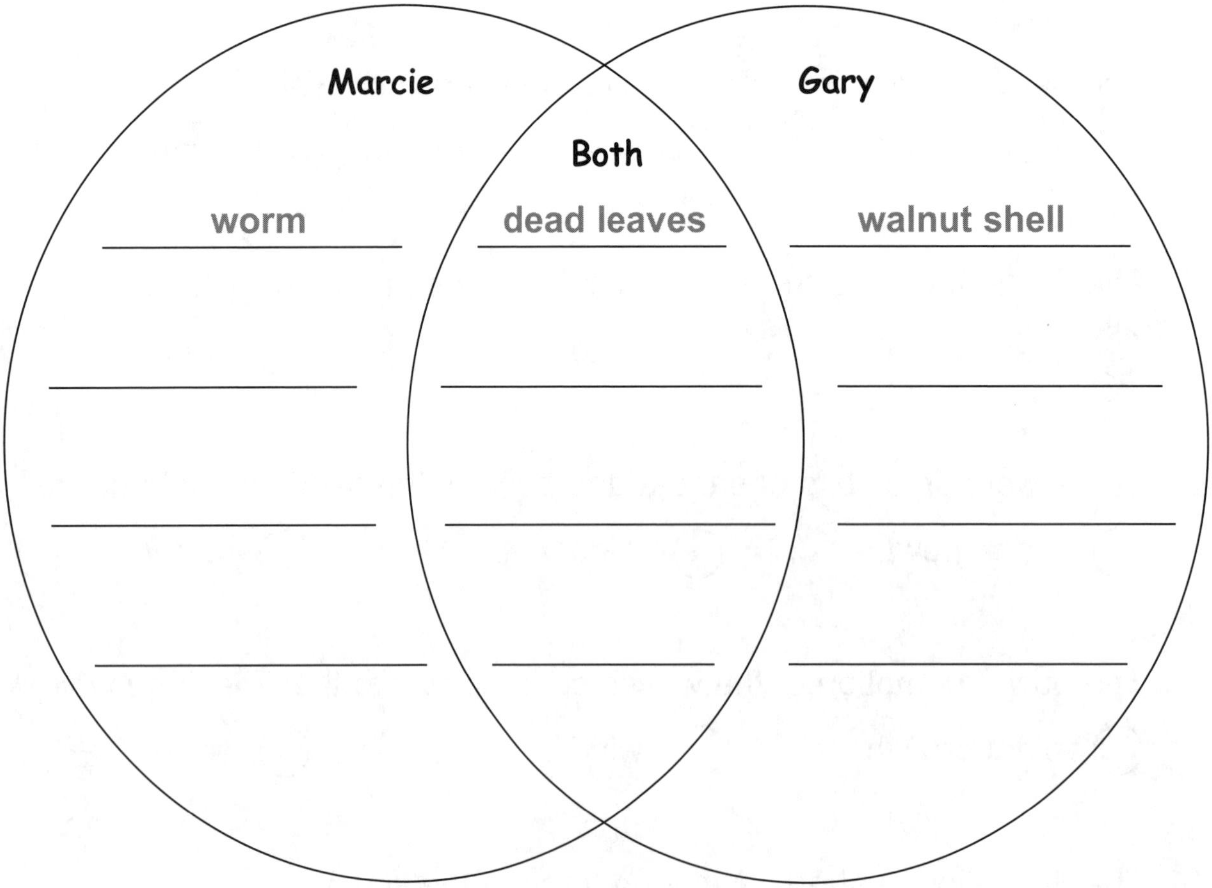

Directions: Answer the following questions using the information in the completed Venn diagram on page 132.

1. Name one thing Marcie found that Gary did not find.

____

2. Name one thing Gary found that Marcie did not find.

____

3. List two items that both Marcie and Gary found in their cups of soil.

   a. ____

   b. ____

4. What item was never part of a living organism?

____

5. Who found the item?

____

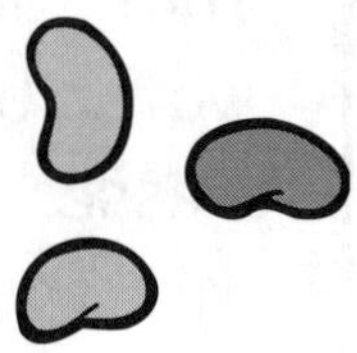

Directions: Read the information about Jesse below. Use the information to help you answer the questions on the next page.

Jesse was helping her mother plant tomatoes. Jesse was surprised to see that it was hard for her mother to dig into the ground as her mother prepared the soil. Jesse's mother pointed to the different layers in the clump she just dug and explained the layers to Jesse. This is what the clump looked like:

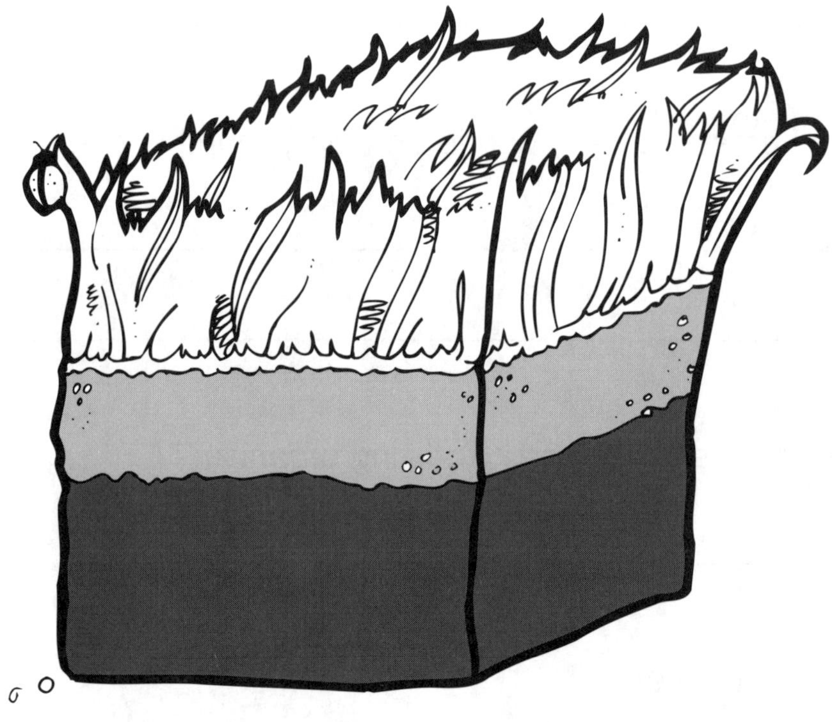

Mom explained that the sandy layer would not hold the water that the plants needed to live and that the clay layer would hold water but is too compact (solid) for the roots to push through. Jesse helped her mother mix material from the compost pile into the layers of the ground to add nutrients to the soil in the garden plot. Mom smiled as she told Jesse that they were adding an invisible ingredient to the soil that would help the plants grow.

Directions: Use the information on page 134 to answer the following questions about the garden. Use a completely filled circle to mark your answer choice.

1. Why is it difficult for plants to grow in all sandy soil?

   ◯ The soil holds too much water.
   ◯ The soil doesn't hold water.
   ◯ The soil is too hard for the roots to push through.

2. Why is it difficult for plants to grow in all clay soil?

   ◯ It is too dry to grow plants.
   ◯ It is too hard for the plants' roots to push through.
   ◯ It is too soft for the plants' roots to push through.

3. What did Jesse's mother add to the soil to provide nutrients for the plants?

   ◯ sand
   ◯ clay
   ◯ compost

4. Mom smiled as she said she was adding an invisible ingredient to the soil. What was it?

   ◯ water for the plants
   ◯ space for the plants
   ◯ compost for the plants

5. Why do you think the invisible ingredient is important?

   ____

   ____

Directions: The flip chart in the front of Mr. Barnet's classroom showed the life cycle of a butterfly (egg-larva-chrysalis-adult). Mr. Barnet asked the students to compare the life cycle of the butterfly to the life cycle of the frog they wrote about in their science journals at the pond. Use the illustrations from the flip chart and Jenny's journal entry to answer the questions below.

Jenny's Journal Entry April 10
Observing at the Pond

I see some small clear balls about the size of a marble with black swirls in them. They must be gooey because they are sticking to the grass near the edge of the pond. I see different sized tadpoles. Their tails are different sizes. The tadpoles have different numbers of legs. The older the tadpole, the more legs. Mr. B. told us that as tadpoles mature, their tails disappear. I see some adult frogs here with all four legs and no tails.

The Life Cycle of a Butterfly

Stage 1

Stage 2

Stage 3

Stage 4

1. How are the life cycles of the butterfly and the frog the same?

____

____

____

2. How are the life cycles of the butterfly and the frog different?

____

____

____

Directions: The students in Mrs. Brown's class are studying how birds have adapted their beaks to fit their sources of food. The students created the following chart to distinguish the different categories of beaks based on their physical descriptions and how they are used in obtaining food.

Type of Bird Beak	Description of Beak	How Beak Is Used
Seed-eating	Short, thick	Crunching, cracking seeds
Insect-eating	Long, slender, pointed	Picking up insects
Probing	Long, slender	Poking into mud or flowers
Preying	Strong, sharp, hooded	Tearing food apart
Straining	Broad, flat, sieve-like	Straining mud from food
Fish-eating	Long, sharp	Spearing food or catching fish

Directions: Read the descriptions of the birds below. Use the chart on page 137 to help you answer the questions. Use a completely filled circle to mark your answer choice.

1. The woodpecker pounds holes into wood to find insects. What type of beak does it have?

   ○ long, slender, pointed ○ short, thick ○ strong, sharp, hooded

2. The hummingbird uses its beak to gather nectar from flowers. What type of beak does it have?

   ○ preying ○ probing ○ straining

3. The cardinal is a seed-eating bird. How does it use its beak?

   ○ tearing food ○ spearing food ○ crunching, cracking food

4. The heron stabs at small fish with a sharp beak. What type of beak does it have?

   ○ probing ○ fish-eating ○ preying

5. The pelican uses its beak to scoop a large mouthful of fish. Describe its beak.

   ○ broad, flat, sieve-like ○ pouch-like ○ long, slender, pointed

6. The duck uses its beak to separate its food from the mud. What type of beak does it have?

   ○ probing ○ straining ○ preying

7. The owl uses its beak to tear apart its food. What type of beak does it have?

   ○ preying ○ probing ○ straining

Directions: Look at the key. Fill in the circle below each organism for each trait that applies to that organism. Use the information from the key to answer the questions. Use a completely filled circle to mark your answer choice.

 **Keys** are used to sort information.	 **bee**	 **grasshopper**	 **ladybug**	 **spider**
is a living organism	○	○	○	○
has six legs	○	○	○	○
has three body parts	○	○	○	○
has wings	○	○	○	○
has spots on its wings	○	○	○	○

1. Which organism has the least number of characteristics on the key?
   - ○ bee
   - ○ ladybug
   - ○ spider

2. Which organism has all of the characteristics listed on the key?
   - ○ grasshopper
   - ○ ladybug
   - ○ spider

3. What do all of the organisms shown on the key above have in common?
   - ○ They all need food, shelter, water, and space to survive.
   - ○ They only need water to survive.
   - ○ They only need food and water to survive.

Directions: Earth revolves (goes around) the Sun one cycle each year. The seasons change because Earth is tilted on an angle as it goes around the Sun. Our planet stays tilted in the same direction as it completes each orbit.

The following illustration will help you answer the questions below. Use a completely filled circle to mark which season is being described.

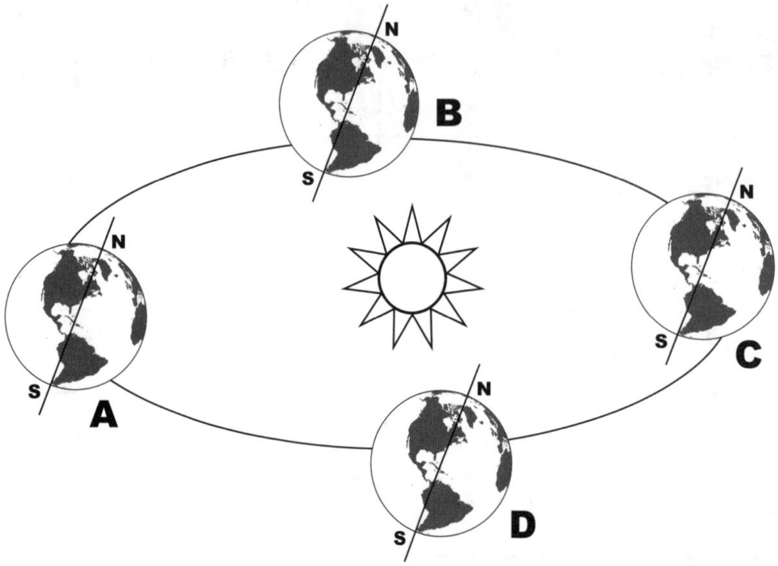

1. When the North Pole is tilted toward the Sun, the days are the longest and warmest.

   ○ Summer ○ Winter ○ Spring

2. Which letter shows Earth with the North Pole tilted toward the Sun?

   ○ A ○ B ○ C

3. When the North Pole tilts away from the Sun, the days are the shortest and the coolest.

   ○ Summer ○ Autumn ○ Winter

4. Which letter shows Earth with the North Pole tilted away from the Sun?

   ○ B ○ C ○ D

Directions: Use a completely filled circle to show which of the following objects can be picked up with a magnet.

		yes	no
1. wooden yo-yo		○	○
2. paper clip		○	○
3. plastic comb	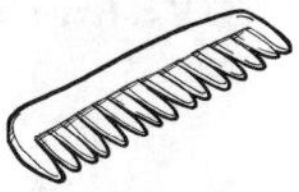	○	○
4. penny		○	○
5. metal screw	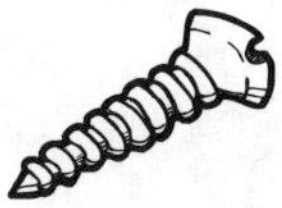	○	○
6. a smaller magnet	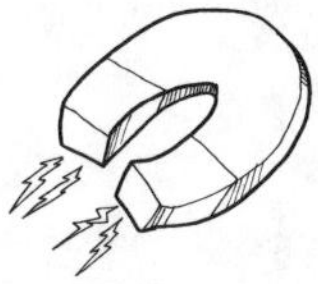	○	○
7. paper		○	○
8. rubber ball	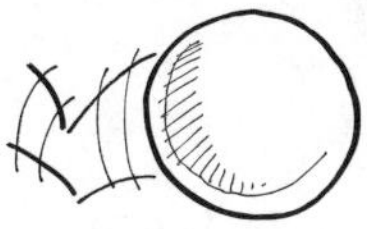	○	○
9. pencil	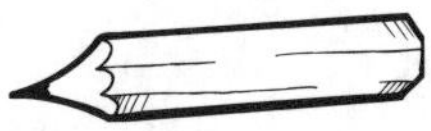	○	○
10. nail		○	○

Directions: The third-grade students were constructing cars for the Car Derby. The rules for the contest were posted on the bulletin board. Maxine ran some test trials with her car. Predict what you think will happen to the distance her car will travel from the bottom of the ramp. Use a completely filled circle to mark you answer choice.

Rules for the Car Derby

All students must:

- construct their cars from the same materials.
- use the same ramp in the contest.
- measure the distance their cars travel from the bottom of the ramp.

	Distance Traveled		
	longer	**shorter**	**no change**
1. Maxine added weight to her car.	○	○	○
2. Maxine sanded the rough edges on her car.	○	○	○
3. Maxine moved the ramp so her car would travel from the smooth floor onto the carpeted area.	○	○	○
4. Maxine launched her car from the ramp onto the rough cement sidewalk.	○	○	○

Directions: Fill in the areas on the chart to identify the missing helpful (positive) or harmful (negative) effects of common forms of technology.

Form of Technology	Helpful (Positive) Effect	Harmful (Negative) Effect
Skateboard		Can be physically injured
Electronic Games	Can be fun and challenging to play	
Computer		May spend too much time on the computer
Scissors	Can be used to cut paper, material, etc.	

Directions: Read the passage, then respond to the questions that follow.

In the early 1900s, all transportation vehicles used the same streets. Cars, bicycles, and horse drawn carriages traveled the same streets and roads together, and accidents were very common. A young inventor named Garrett Augustus Morgan witnessed an accident between a car and a horse-drawn carriage. He invented a T-shaped pole device to help control these accidents. It had three positions: stop, go, and all-directions (everyone waits).

1. What invention is being suggested (inferred) in the reading passage?

___

___

2. What was the cause for Garrett Morgan's invention?

___

___

___

3. Explain the effect of Garrett Morgan's invention.

___

___

___

Directions: Rory told all her friends that she could do a magic trick. In the trick, she said she would pick up a dollar bill with a magnet and two large paper clips. None of her fingers would touch the dollar bill as she lifted it. Draw a picture of how Rory might perform the magic trick. Be sure to label all the parts of your illustration.

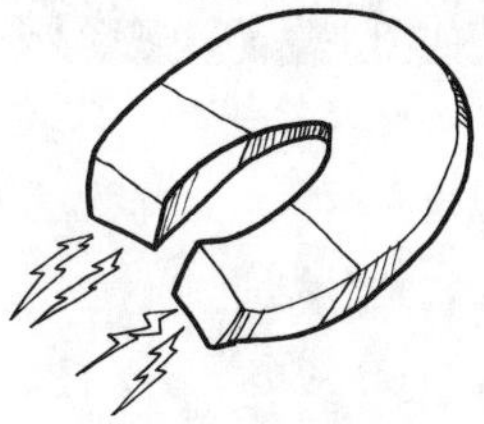

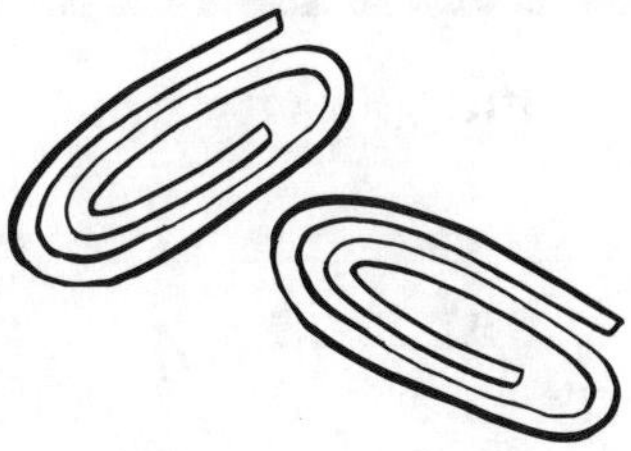

What force makes this trick work? ______________________________

Directions: Keisha recorded the following temperatures for cities in Ohio. Find the range of temperature (high temperature minus low temperature) for each city listed on the chart, then answer the questions below.

Temperatures* for July 14, 2003			
	High	Low	Range for the Day
Columbus	87°	65°	______
Cincinnati	84°	65°	______
Cleveland	81°	64°	______
Dayton	83°	65°	______
Toledo	85°	62°	______
Youngstown	79°	64°	______
Zanesville	86°	62°	______

*temperatures in degrees Fahrenheit

1. What was the highest temperature for the day? ______
2. What was the lowest temperature for the day? ______
3. Which city had the greatest range in temperature for the day?

   ______

4. Which city had the least range in temperature for the day?

   ______

Directions: Dr. Jim was a very interesting science teacher. He always wanted the students to think about things they did in the lab. On the first day of school, he wanted the students to help decide what rules were important in the lab. He made the first rule each year **"Report problems to the teacher immediately!"** Then, he provided examples of things that might happen in the class, followed by questions to help students identify other important rules.

1. Today the class will be launching film canister rockets. How will they protect their eyes?

   ____

   ____

2. Michael chose the plastic beaker instead of the glass one to collect the soil sample from the playground. Why?

   ____

   ____

3. Lorenzo dropped his soil sample when Jacob ran into him. What went wrong here?

   ____

   ____

4. The fire alarm went off when the candle experiment fell on the counter. What should the students know how to do?

   ____

   ____

5. The class left the seeds, soil, and pots scattered throughout the lab. What should they do before the class is over?

   ____

   ____

Directions: The third graders at Central Elementary School created a calendar to show the phases of the moon during March. Use the data illustrated on their calendar to answer the questions below.

Phases of the Moon

New Moon

First Quarter Moon

Full Moon

Last Quarter Moon

March

Sunday	Monday	Tuesday	Wednesday	Thursday	Friday	Saturday
			1 	2	3	4
5	6	7	8	9 	10	11
12	13	14	15	16 	17	18
19	20 First Day of Spring	21	22	23 	24	25
26	27	28	29	30 	31	

1. How many new moons occurred during the month? __________

2. On which day of the week was there a full moon? __________

3. Did the first day of spring come before or after the first quarter moon? __________

4. How many phases are there in the moon cycle? __________

5. Record the dates for new moons.

____

6. What moon phase follows a new moon?

____

Directions: Miss Science told the third graders that they would experience several types of scientific activities during the school year. They would **explore** (use all of their senses), **investigate** (find questions and answers), and **experiment** (develop a hypothesis about an event or topic, test it, and compare the results of the test to their hypothesis about what they thought would happen). Use a completely filled circle to show what type of activity is being described in each example below.

1. Leon wonders why the sky is blue.

   ○ explore ○ investigate ○ experiment

2. Marlene smells a strange odor on the playground.

   ○ explore ○ investigate ○ experiment

3. Steven said the soil in Cup A felt lumpier than the soil in Cup B.

   ○ explore ○ investigate ○ experiment

4. Shana wants to test her prediction that the cup of water on the sunny windowsill will evaporate faster than the one in the closet.

   ○ explore ○ investigate ○ experiment

5. Toby asked Mr. Baker why the water at the beach is warm at night.

   ○ explore ○ investigate ○ experiment

6. Celeste thinks that her classmates would rather go on a field trip to the zoo than to the park. She is taking a poll to see if she is correct.

   ○ explore ○ investigate ○ experiment

Directions: Look at the table below to help you evaluate the results of the water evaporation experiment conducted by Groups 1 and 2.

	Group 1	Group 2
Day 1	1 cup water	1 cup water
Day 2	1 cup water	$\frac{3}{4}$ cup water
Day 3	1 cup water	$\frac{3}{4}$ cup water
Day 4	$\frac{3}{4}$ cup water	$\frac{1}{4}$ cup water
Day 5	$\frac{1}{2}$ cup water	empty

1. Did both groups begin their experiments with equal amounts of water?

____

2. Did the water evaporate at the same rate for both groups?

____

3. How are the experiment results different between the two groups?

____

4. Write a possible explanation for the different results. Use supporting information in your response.

____

____

____

____

Directions: Read the passage below carefully. Write complete sentences to respond to the questions about it.

Rachel Carson was a marine biologist who worked with the United States Fish and Wildlife Service. During her lifetime, she noticed that the usual spring sounds, such as the humming of insects and the buzzing of bees, were missing in nature. She wanted to know why this was happening. Ms. Carson found out that the pesticides and other chemicals that the farmers were using to produce more crops were harming the lakes, the rivers, and the insect populations. Her research showed that chemicals used to benefit society in one way could harm nature in other ways. Rachel Carson's work pointed out the need for a national protection agency to watch over the environment.

1. What sparked Rachel Carson's curiosity about the environment?

____

____

2. What created the problem Rachel Carson investigated?

____

____

3. How did Rachel Carson's work benefit the environment?

____

____

____

Directions: Clark Elementary School is hosting a Science in Action night for the community. Below is the list of the local scientists who are holding workshops and the specific topics of those workshops. Which career workshop would be of most interest to the following people attending the event? Use a completely filled circle to mark your answer choice.

Name	Career	Topic
Tom Jakes	Air Pollution Inspector	Pollen and Spring Allergies
Meg Morris	City Planner	The New Civic Park
Carrie Jones	Geologist	Rock Formations of the Local Area

1. Lois wants to learn more about the rock formations in the area.

○ Geologist ○ City Planner ○ Air Pollution Inspector

2. Gene wants to find out if there will be a place to play tennis in the new park.

○ Geologist ○ City Planner ○ Air Pollution Inspector

3. Ralph has allergies and is interested in learning how the pollen in the air is counted.

○ Geologist ○ City Planner ○ Air Pollution Inspector

4. Mr. Philips donated money for recreational equipment at the new park site.

○ Geologist ○ City Planner ○ Air Pollution Inspector

Congratulations

To: ______________________

You have successfully completed

Ready, Set, Show What You Know®

3rd Grade

Parent/Teacher: ______________________

Date: ______________________